AF395163

IN
YOUR
FACE

PAUL TREVOR

IN YOUR FACE

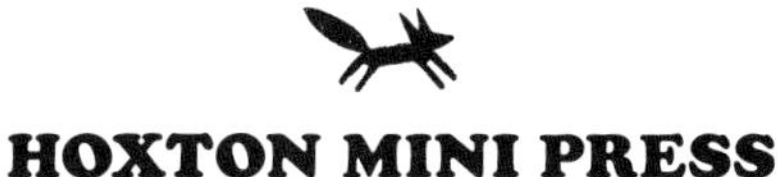

HOXTON MINI PRESS

For Salila and Prasadam

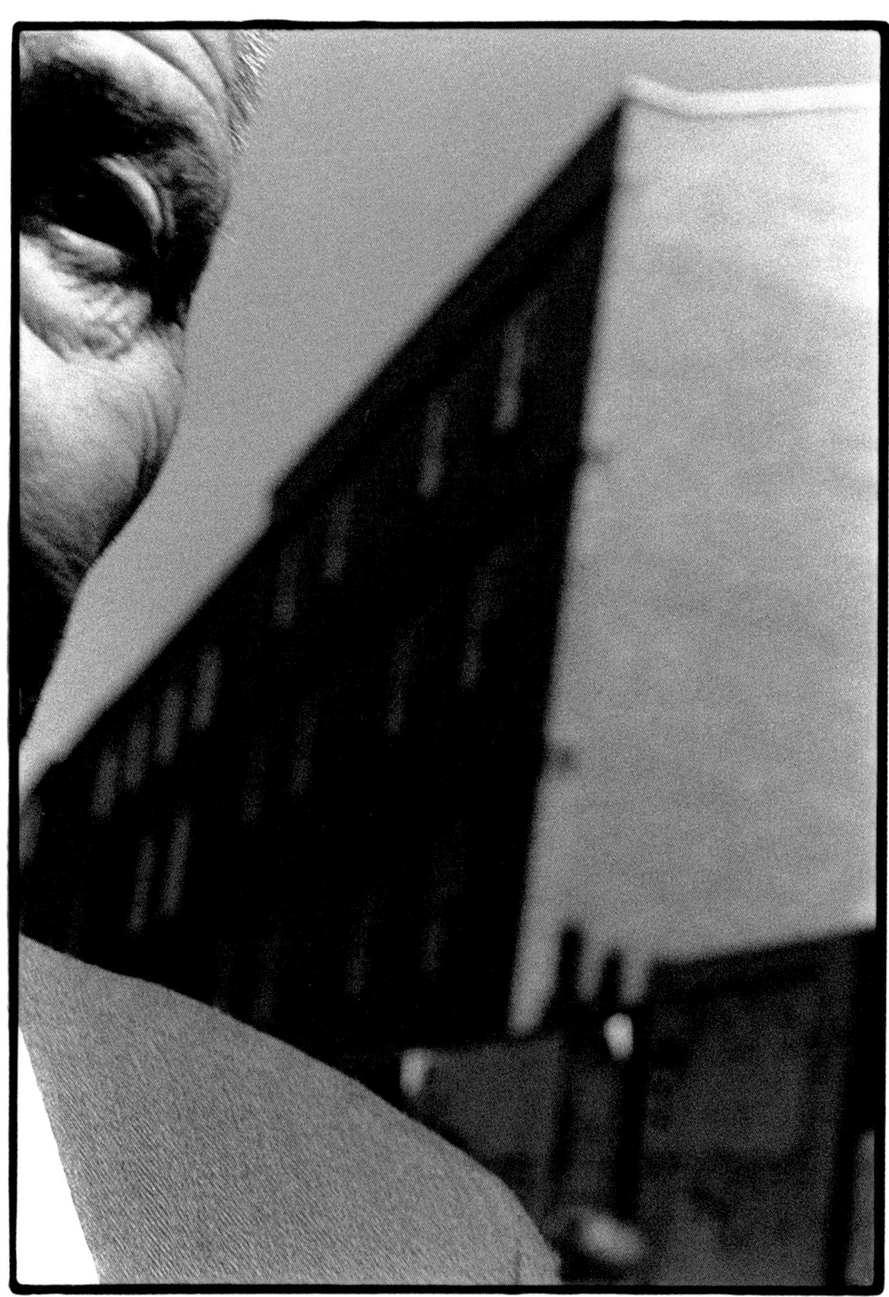

INTRODUCTION

by Stephen McLaren

Several years ago Paul Trevor showed me some handmade *In Your Face* book dummies and I was instantly captivated. The energy and the emotions I sensed in these close-up impromptu portraits, made in Brick Lane and the nearby City of London between 1977 and 1992, was enthralling.

At the time I was compiling *Photographers Sketchbooks*, an anthology of photographers' works-in-progress and I was hunting for bodies of work that felt somehow incomplete or deserving of more attention. Although Paul's project had been exhibited in London at the Royal Festival Hall in 1994, an accompanying book had not been forthcoming and so the work had failed to reach the audience it deserved. I was pleased to be able to include extracts from his dummies in the anthology. Nevertheless, here at last we have the proper vessel for viewing this seminal work of documentary photography in its entirety, as conceived and edited by the photographer.

Why is this body of work 'seminal'? The answer is that Paul Trevor placed his camera so incredibly close up to passers-by on the street that the results amount to a startling new category of photographs. He did this with a 35mm film camera, a bog-standard 50mm lens, and used only available light. He had discovered this simple combination would offer images with the depth and perspective that matched the optics of the human eye – thus creating a feeling of intimate space. Paul's imaginative leap was to get close, and closer still, and use his lightning-fast reflexes to capture a sliver of time as it passed across a person's face. The project demonstrates that with very simple tools the canniest photographer can find unexpected ways of showing us something new.

If our faces are the greatest signifiers of our individuality then the individuals
Paul Trevor dodged and weaved around in the 1980s are seen here in full
relief. Pores, wrinkles, eyelashes, lips, hair products and jewellery tell us much
of the people he encountered. Pick a face and look, and look again and try
to imagine the stories that lie behind the images. Are they locals or just passing
through, immigrants or Cockneys, late for work or early for a date, just
getting by or living large? So much detail to look at, so many questions with
answers hinted at but never delivered.

Paul Trevor never tells us what to think about these people, why would
he? But we do know that he picked the neighbouring Brick Lane and
City of London to alert us to a gulf that opened up between these ancient
commercial districts in the 1980s. On the eastern flank, Brick Lane,
historically a neighbourhood of immigrants, street-traders, breweries and
bakeries. On the western edge, The City, an ancient metropolitan quarter
which worshipped Mammon. As a recession descended, the clickety-clacks
of Brick Lane's sewing machines became muted, the breweries were
moth-balled and many of the denizens of one of Britain's most enervating
streets either left or fell into poverty. Meanwhile The City was cranking
it up a gear, the banks were unleashed and go-getters from Essex, the
Home Counties and the wider world started rolling into Liverpool Street
station with easy-wash suits and a trojan work ethic. On both neighbour-
hoods' market forces were unleashed and Paul found two sets of inhabitants
to focus on, with rapidly diverging life chances and ethical norms.

As I turn each page I find myself looking for a trace of the man behind
the lens, trying to work out how he managed to carry out such an 'inside job'
at 12 inches' distance. The young man in The City who spurts blood from
his nose, the young boy in Brick Lane whose face is pulled until his gums bulge,
the doll-like young woman whose tongue pops out just at the right moment,

how did Paul find and photograph these wonderful creatures and what was motivating him?

'The work demanded that I photograph strangers very close-up without engaging with them. It meant working surreptitiously. I found this approach created a tension in the photos between physical intimacy and emotional detachment. I was fascinated by the results – objective images that were subjective at the same time. That was a new experience.'

Paul Trevor is circumspect about some of the specifics of his work for the project. He may be a spirit-like vapour behind that intrusive 50mm lens. But peering closely at the image of the horse in The City it's possible to see the photographer at work reflected in the animal's eye.

Leaving aside the photographer and his art for a moment, I hope you'll savour all the kisses, fag draws, punches, bloody noses and proper characters that career through this seminal piece of documentary photography and reflect on the market forces that drew Paul Trevor to them in the first instance.

May 2020

The City, 1989

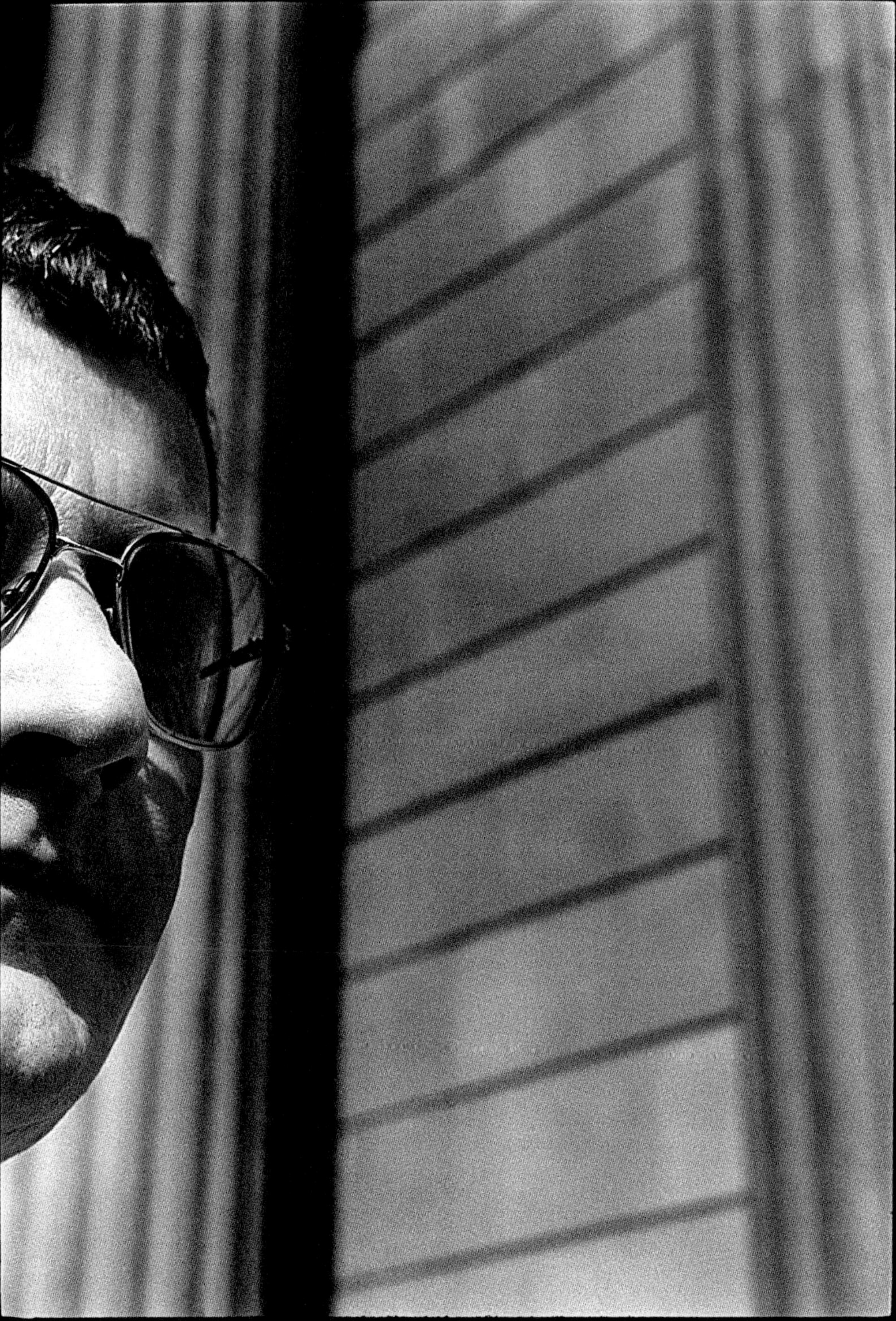

Brick Lane, 1991

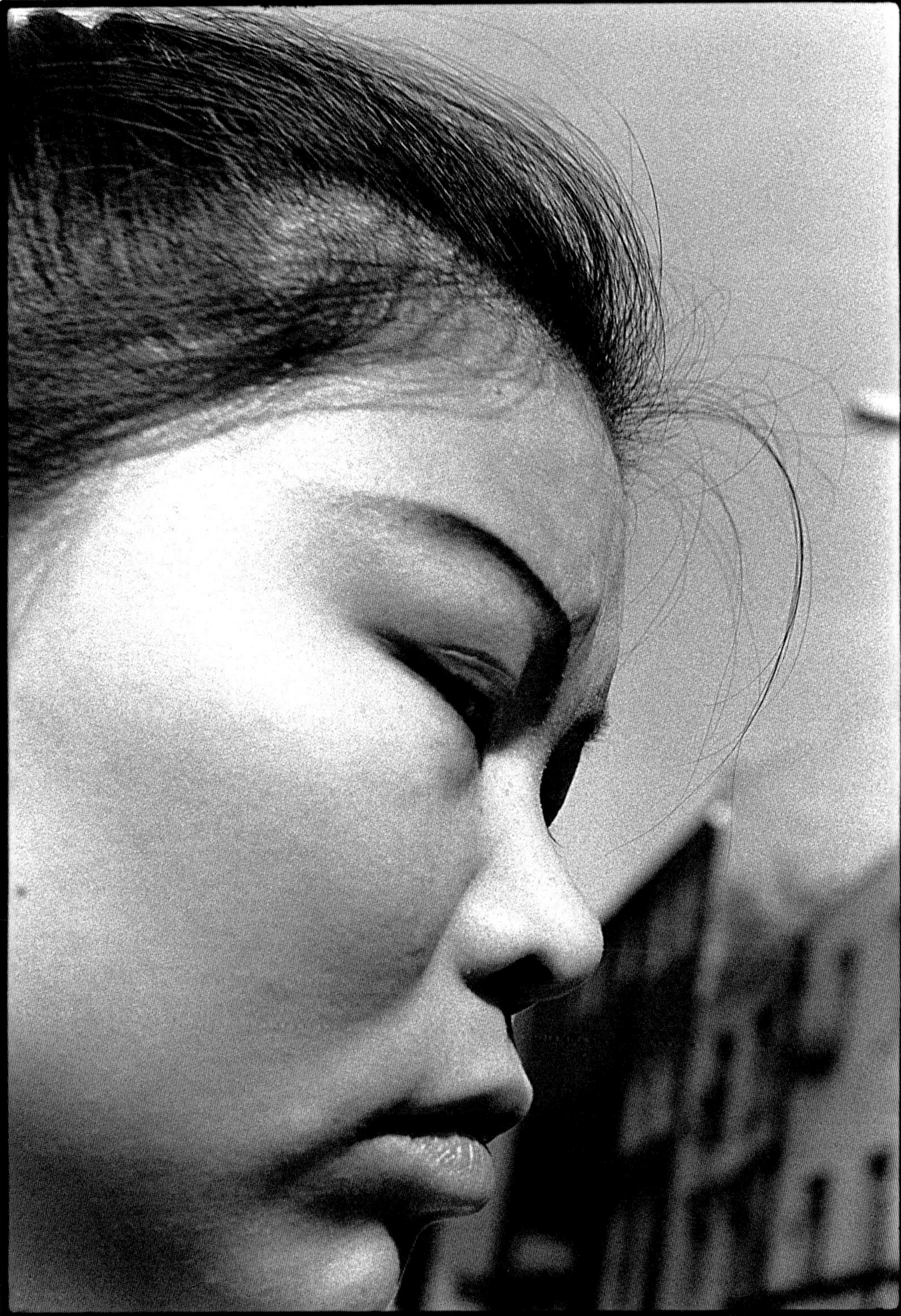

The City, 1989

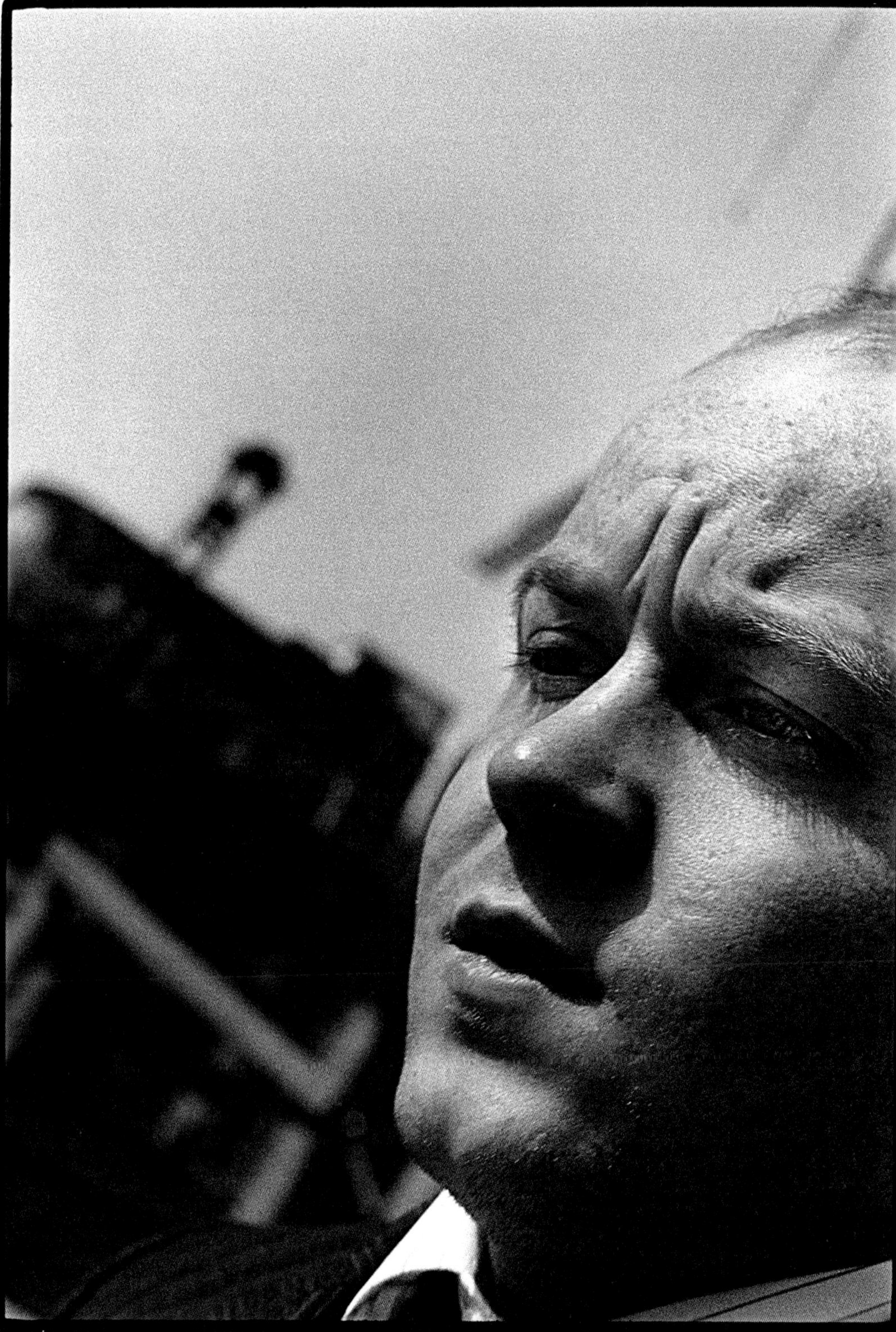

Brick Lane, 1977

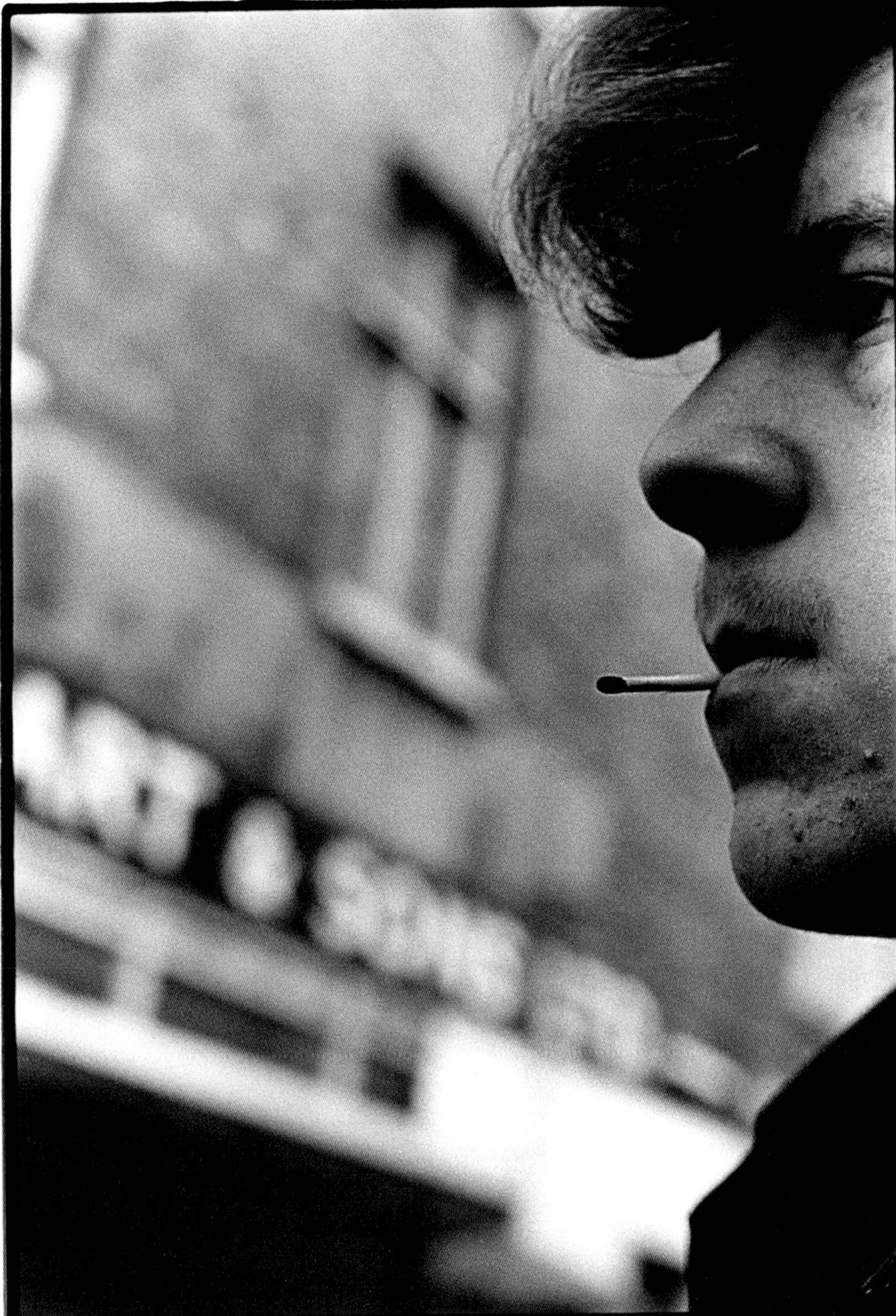

The City, 1989

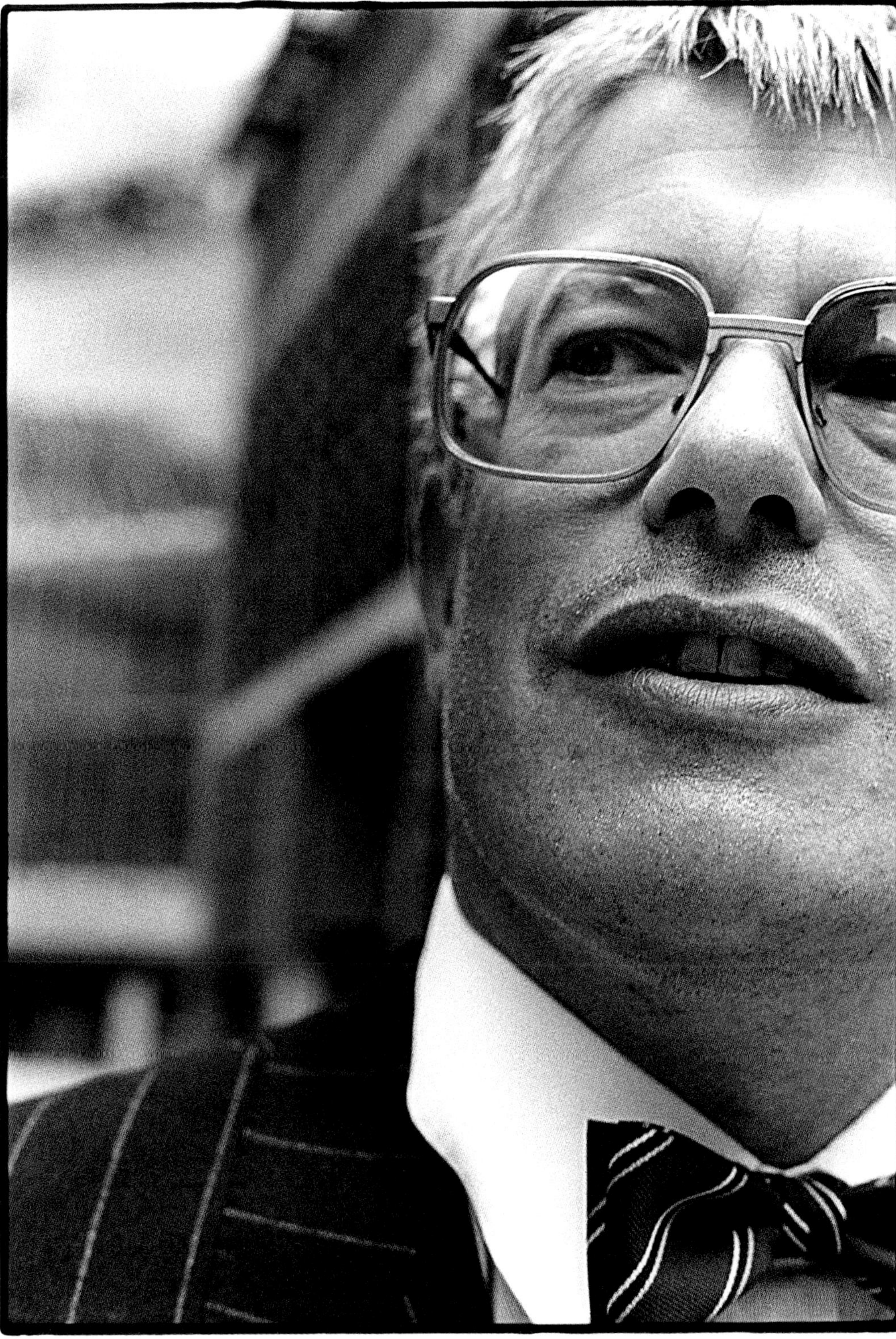

Brick Lane, 1992

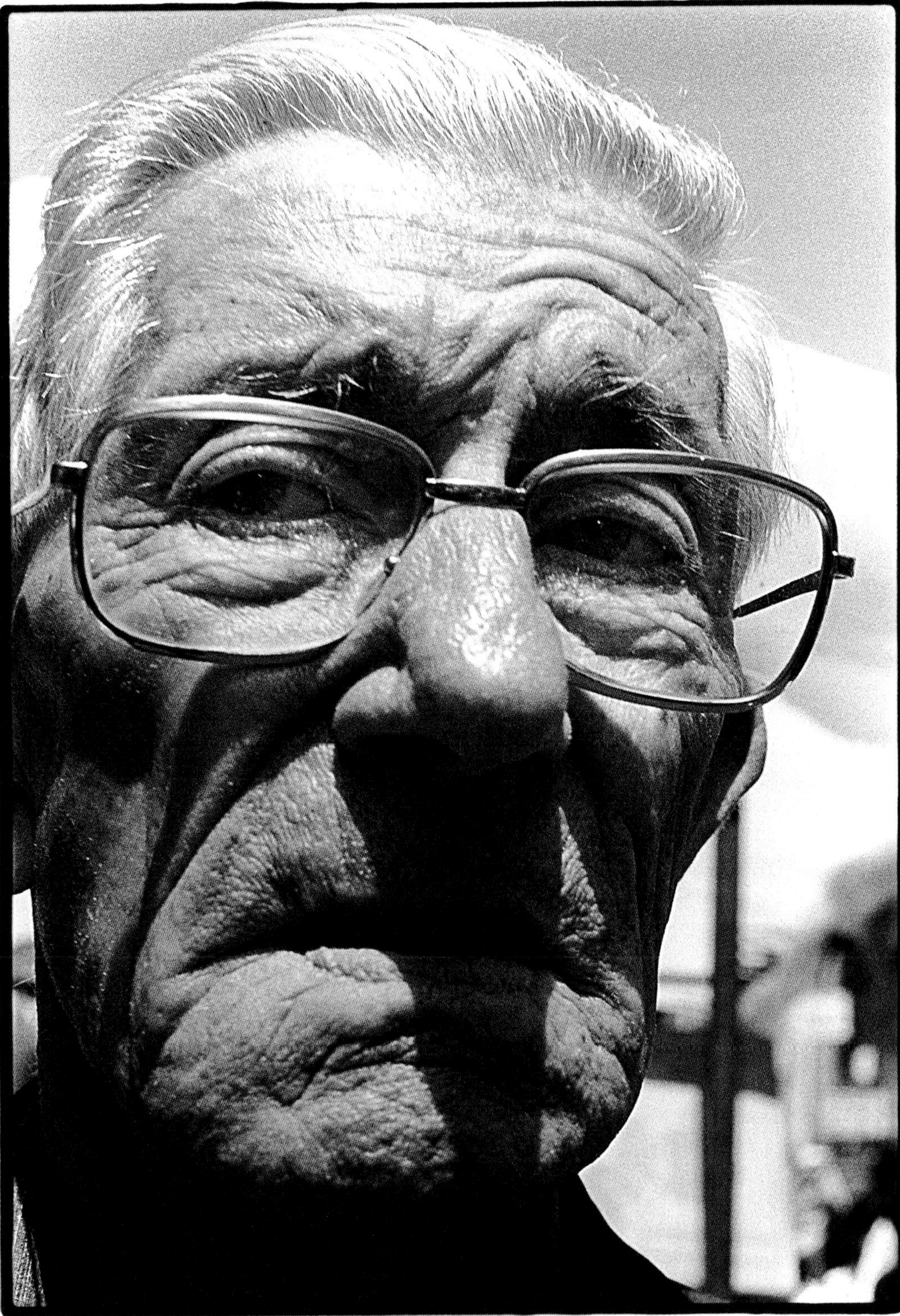

The City, 1989

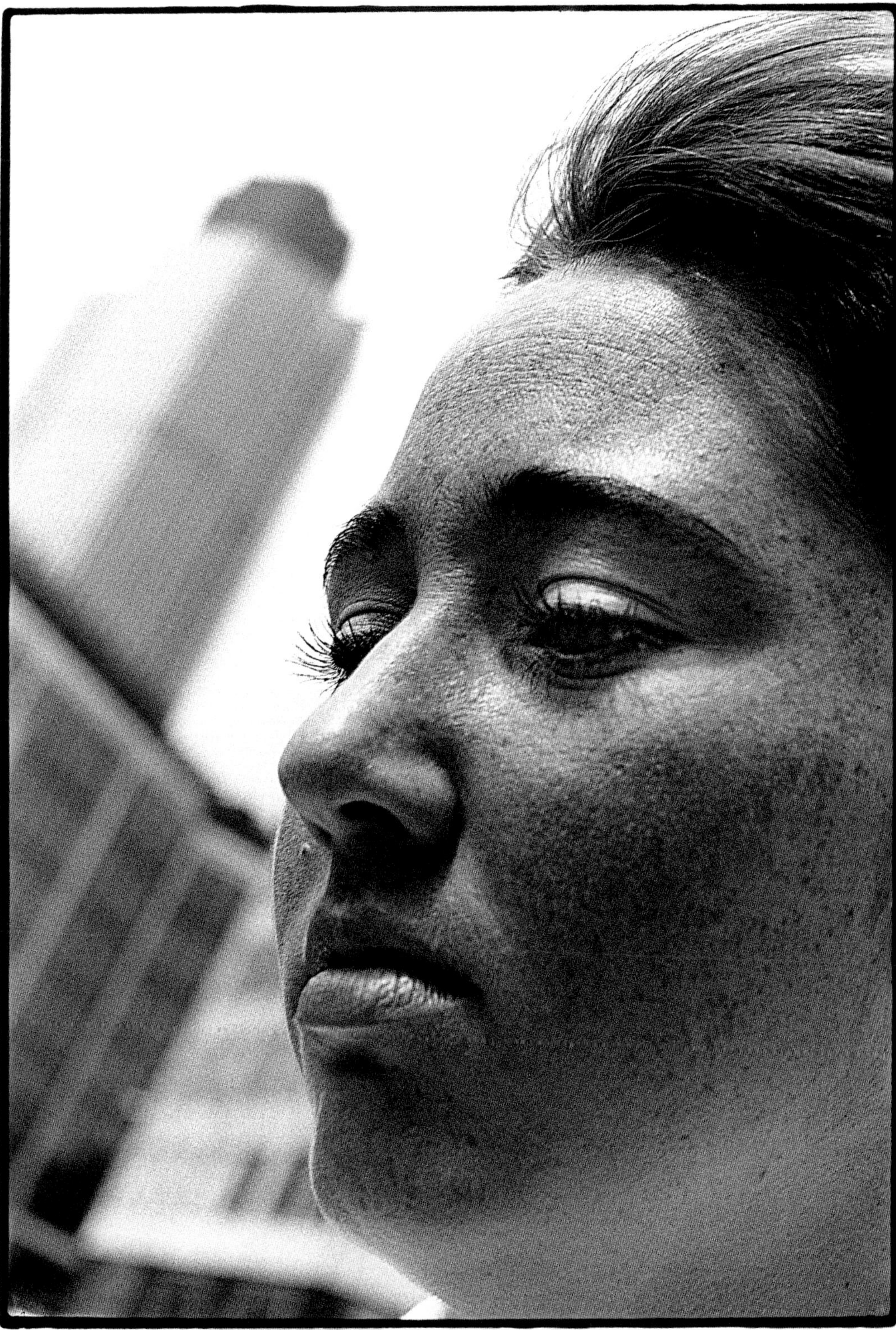

Brick Lane, 1982

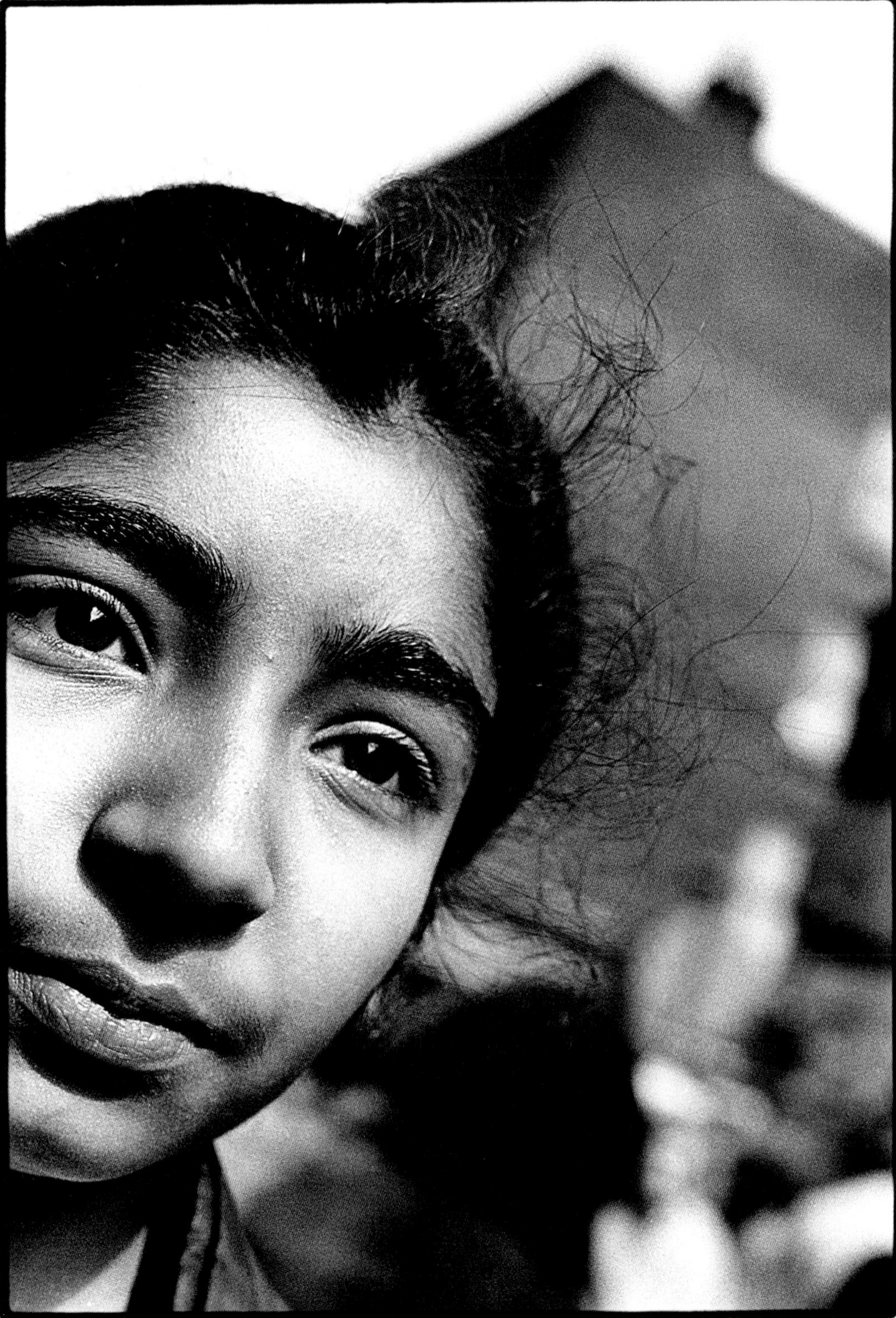

The City, 1989

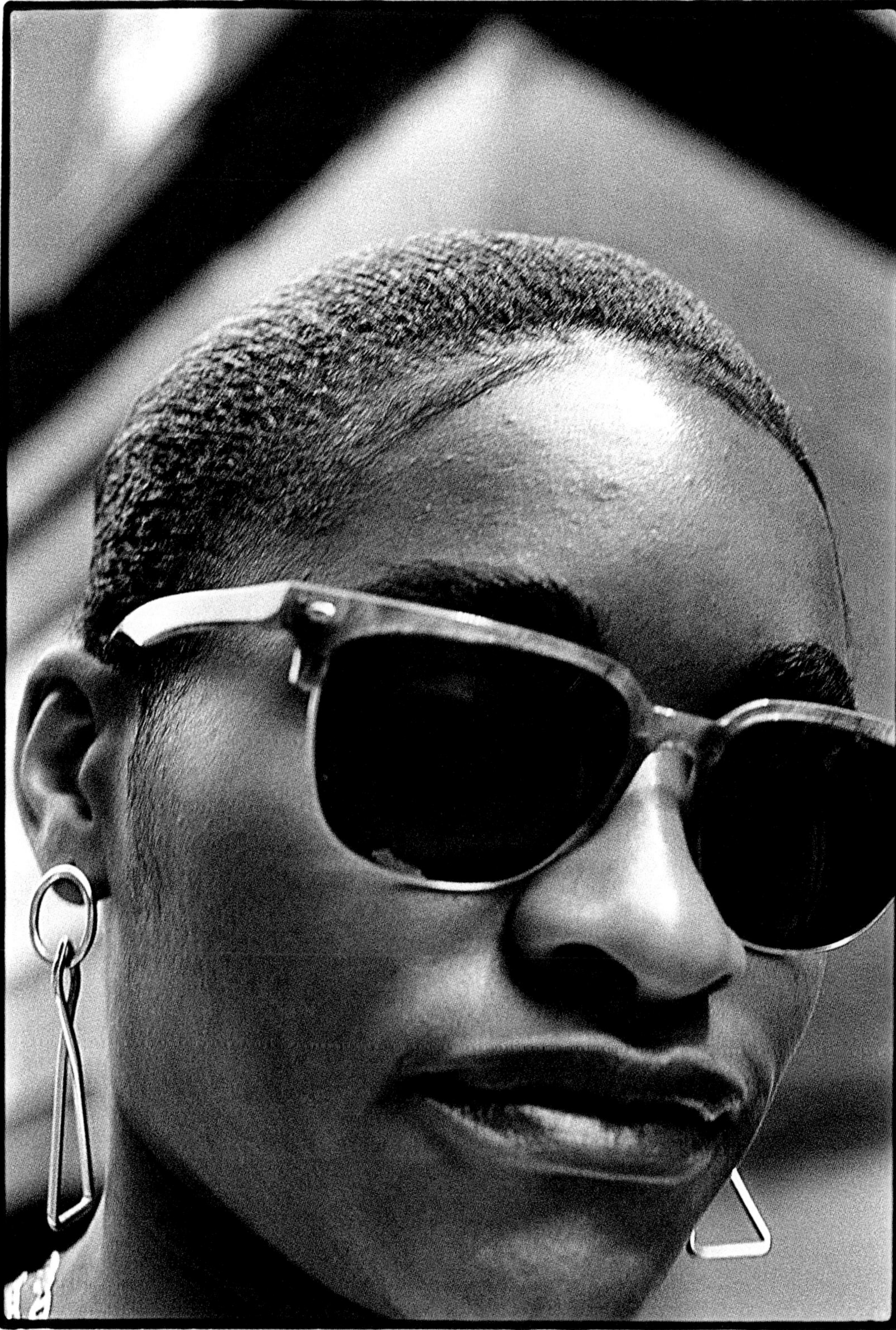

Brick Lane, 1982

Overleaf: The City, 1989

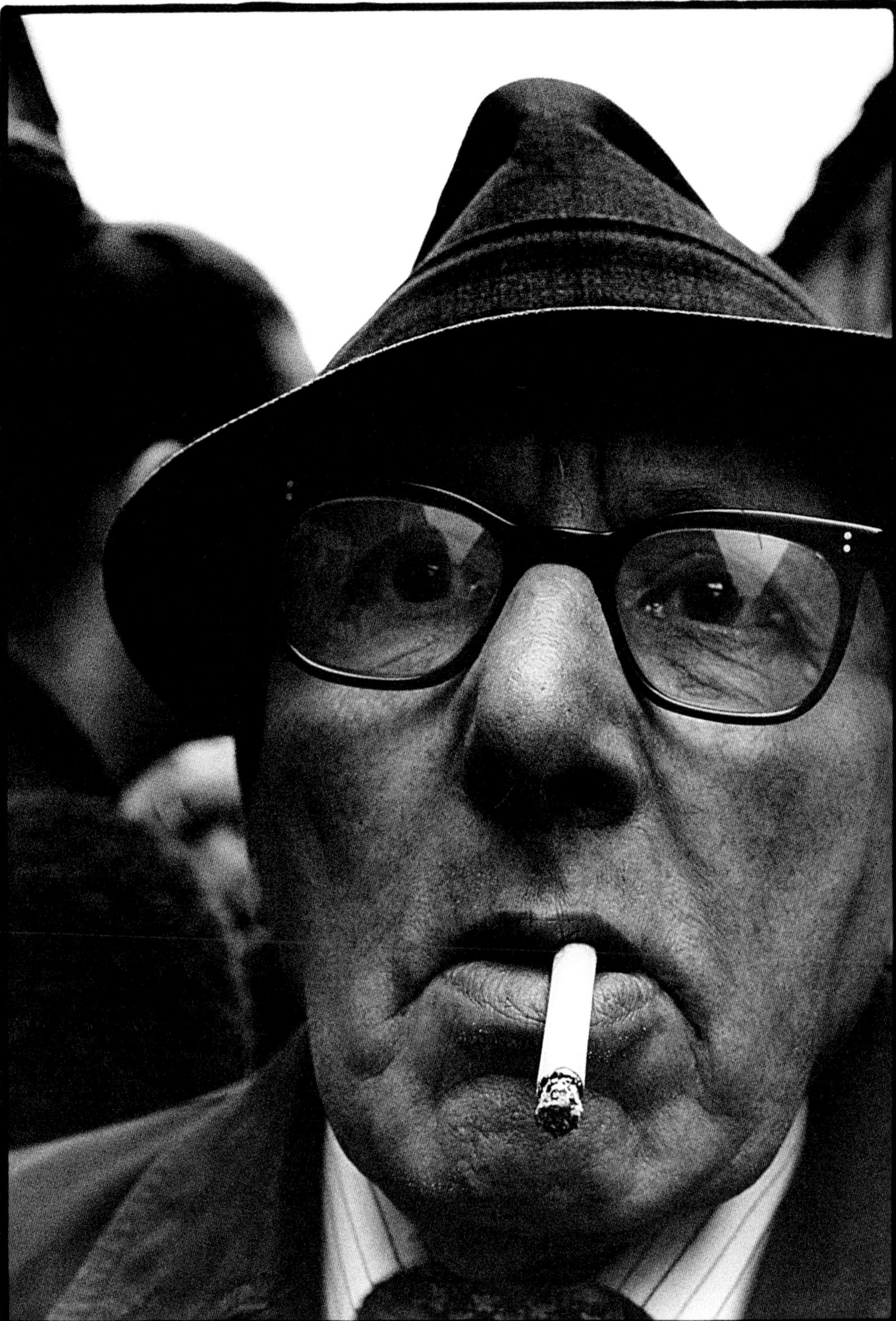

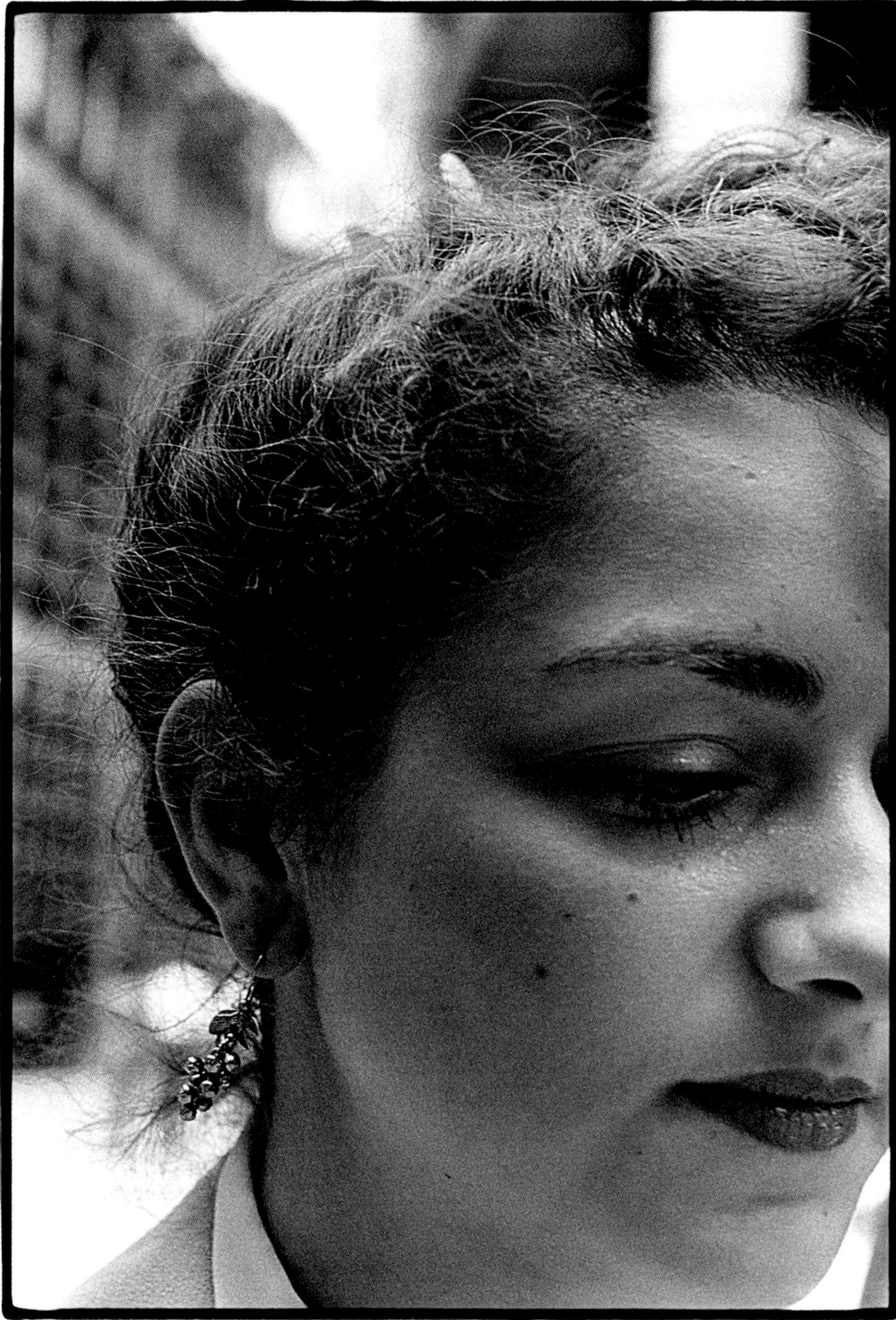

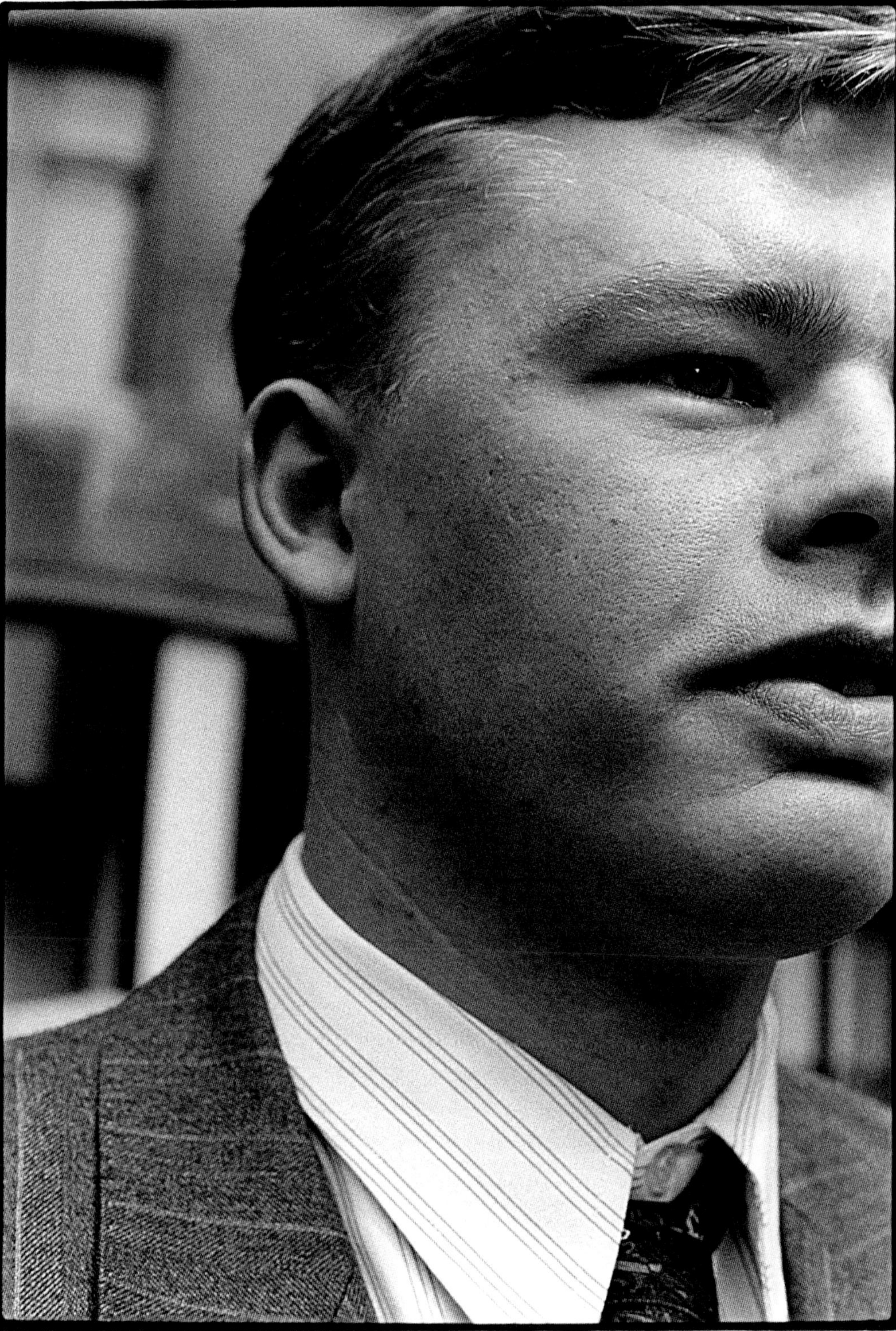

Brick Lane, 1992

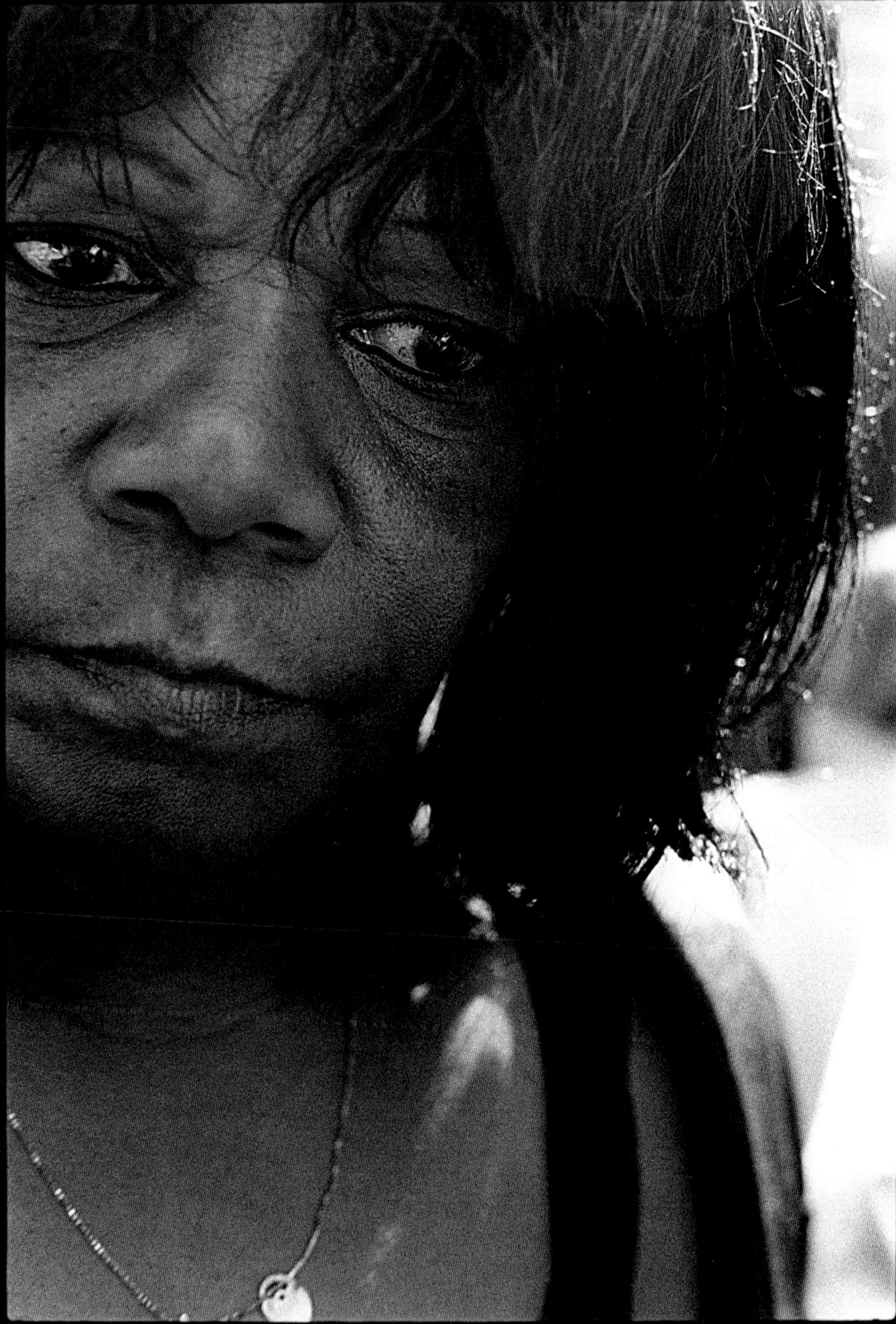

The City, 1989

Overleaf: Brick Lane, 1977 and 1982

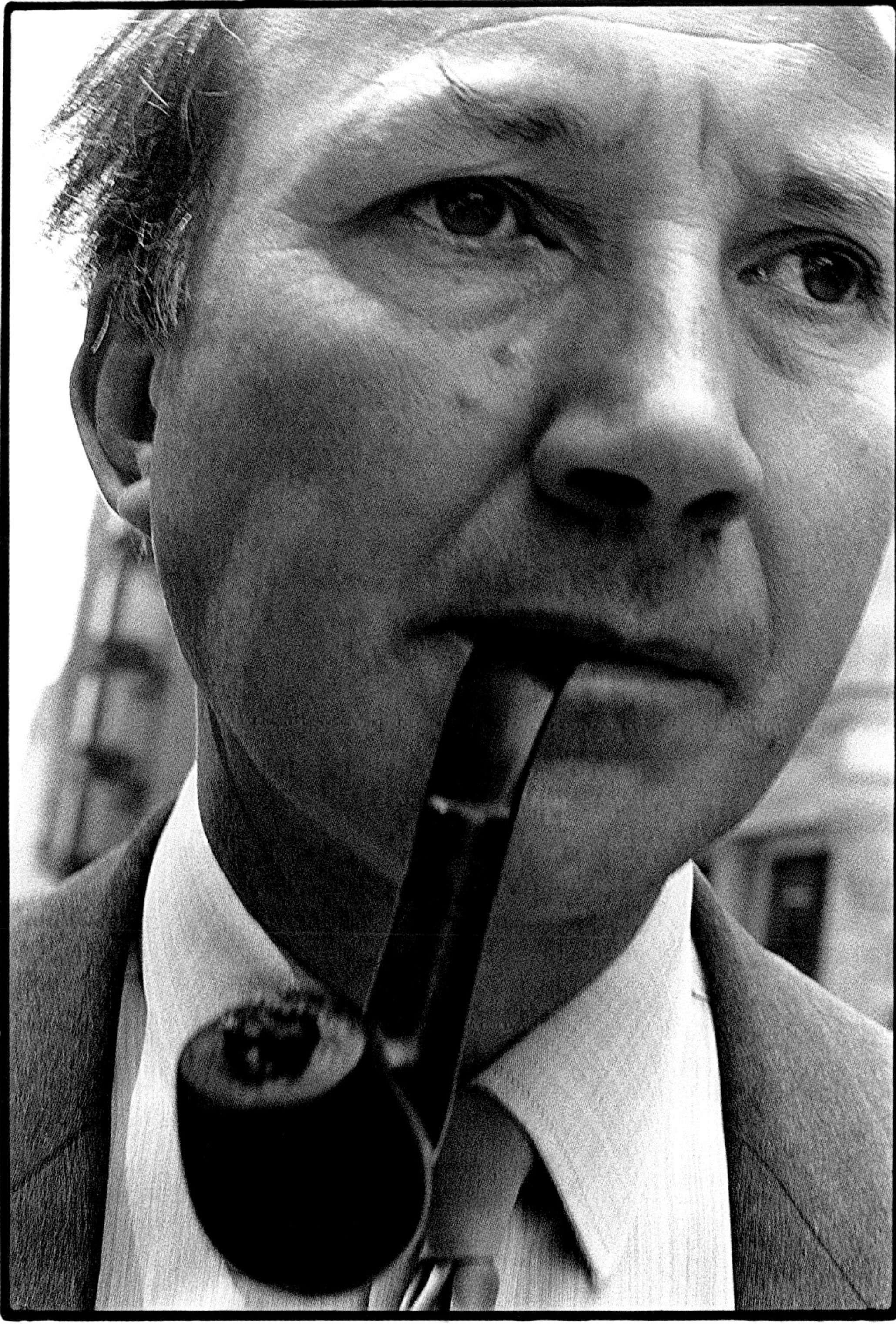

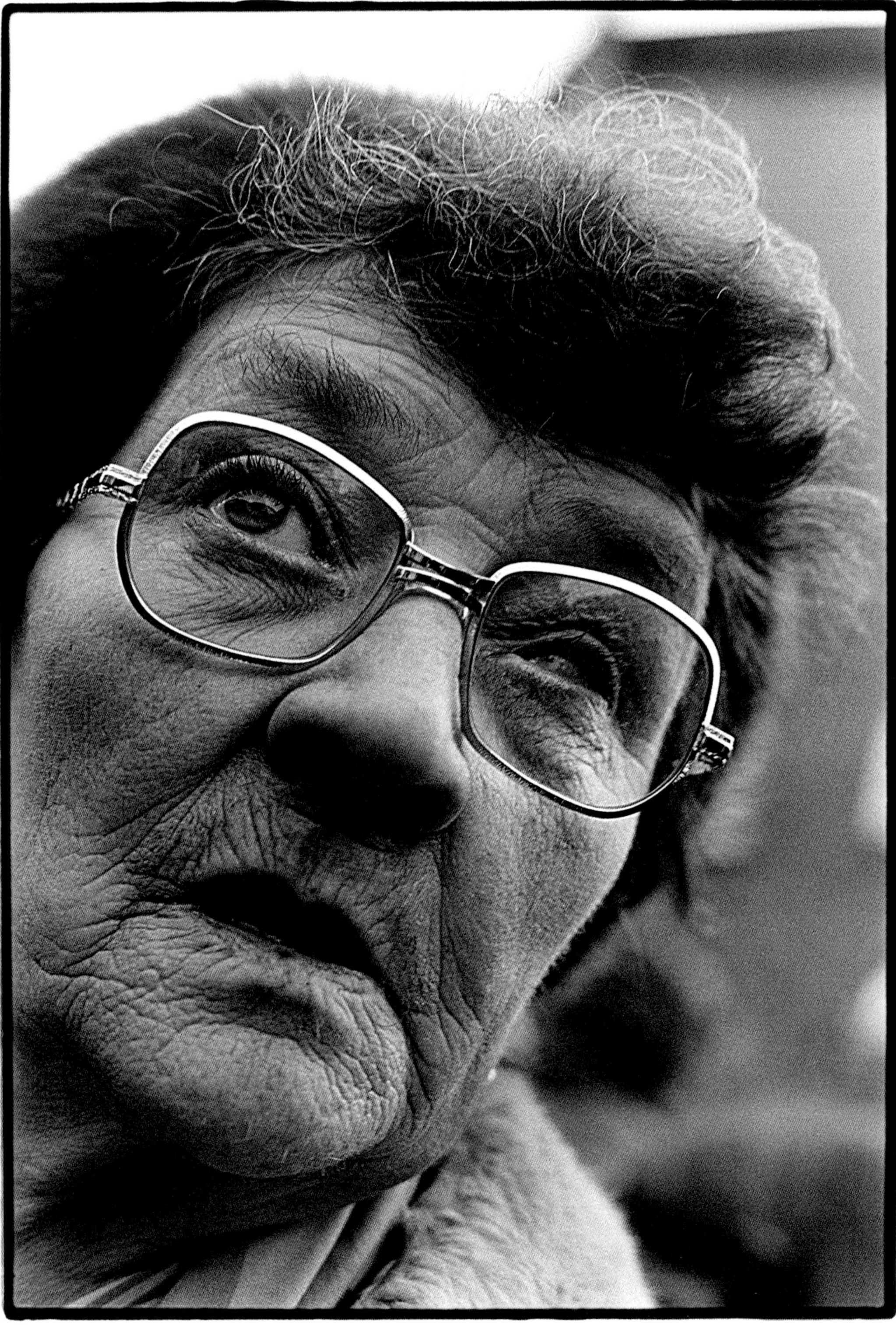

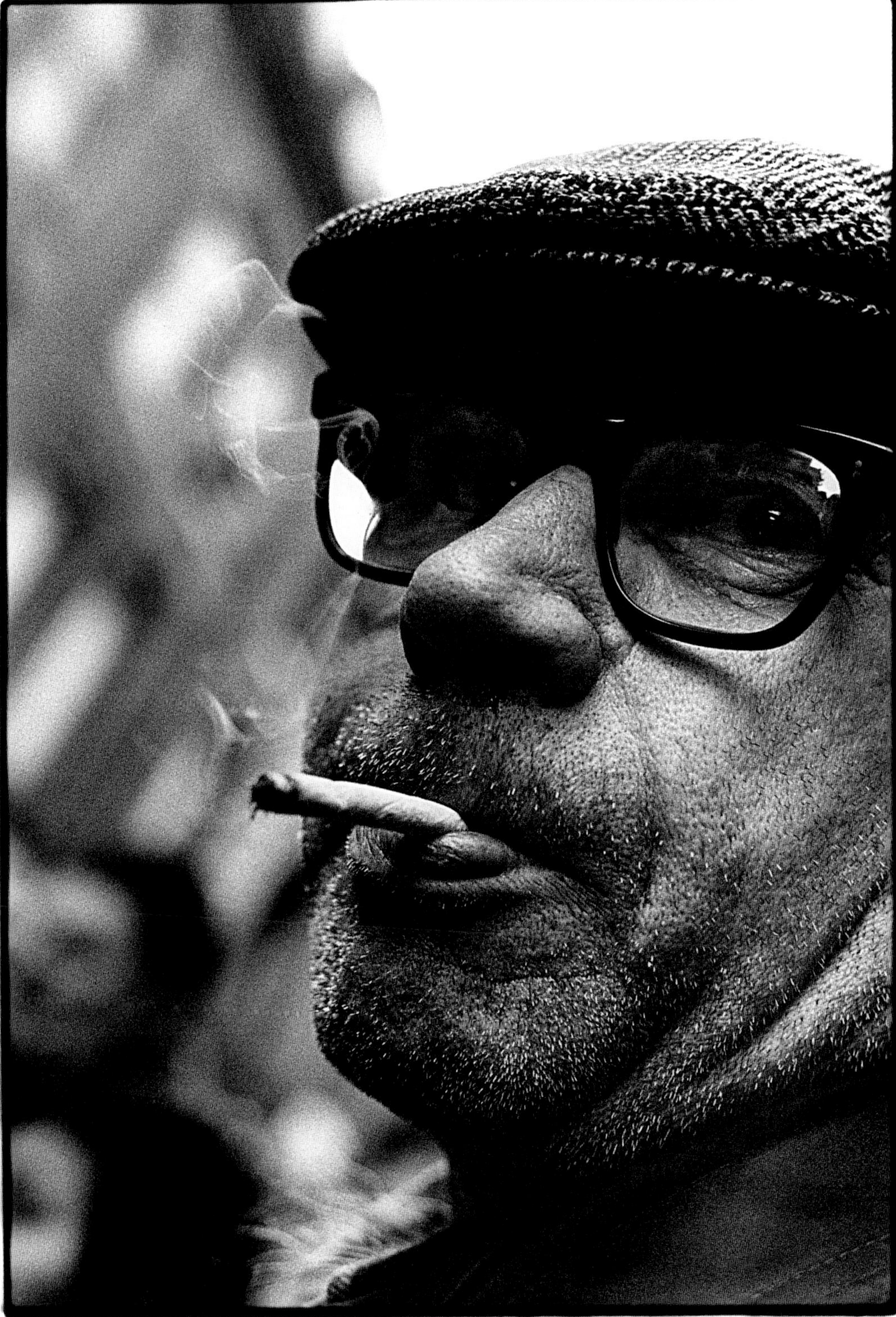

The City, 1989

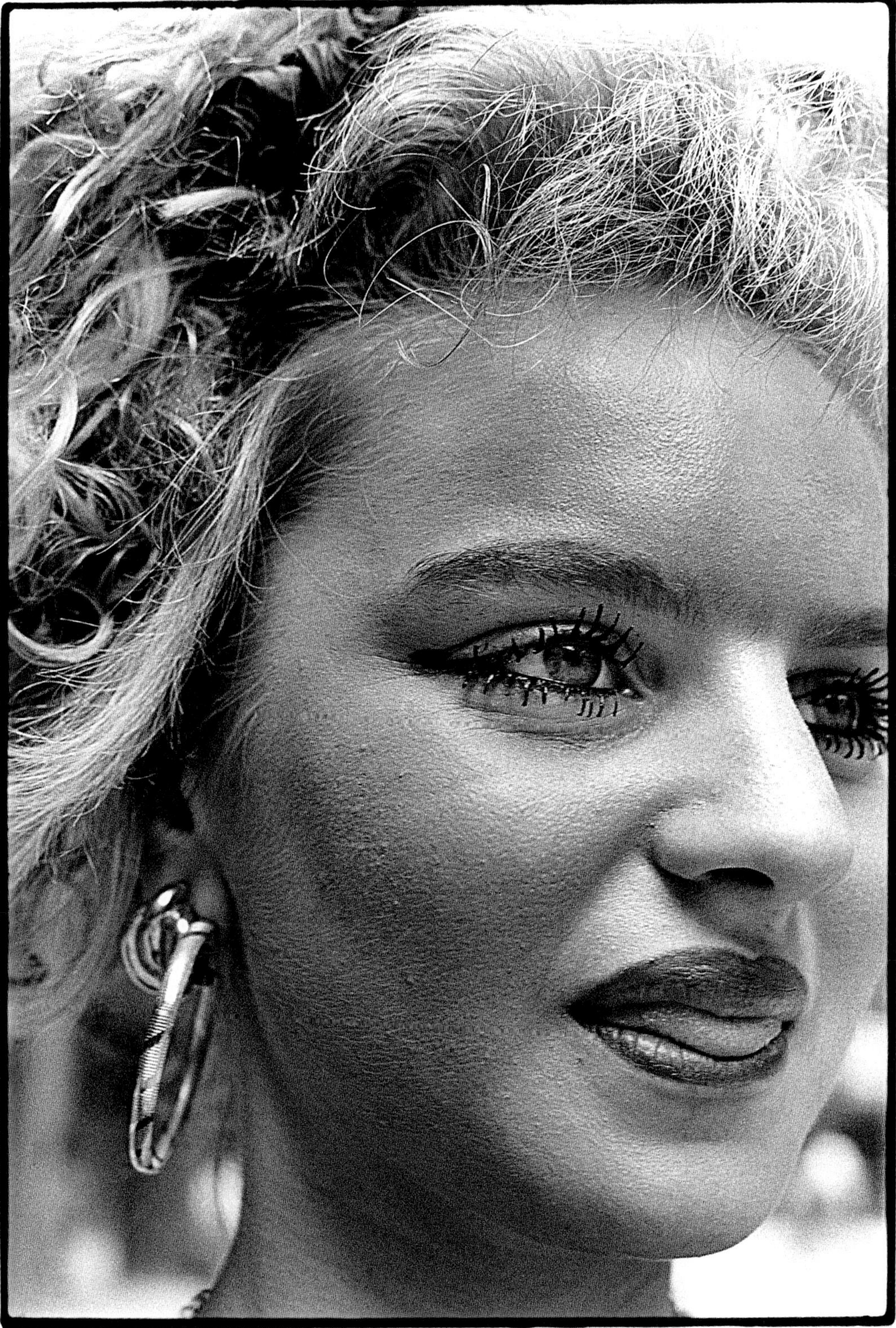

Brick Lane, 1989

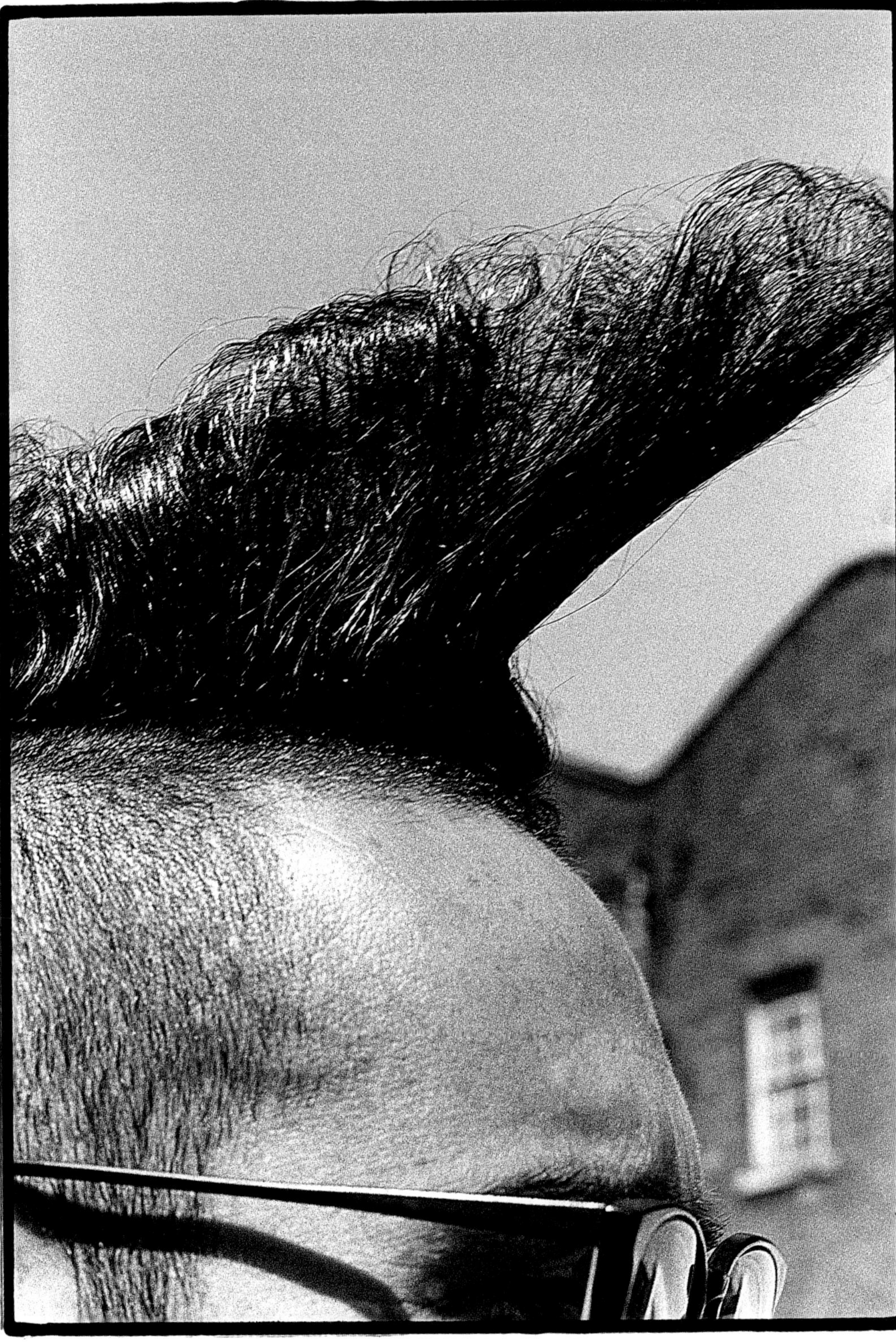

The City, 1989

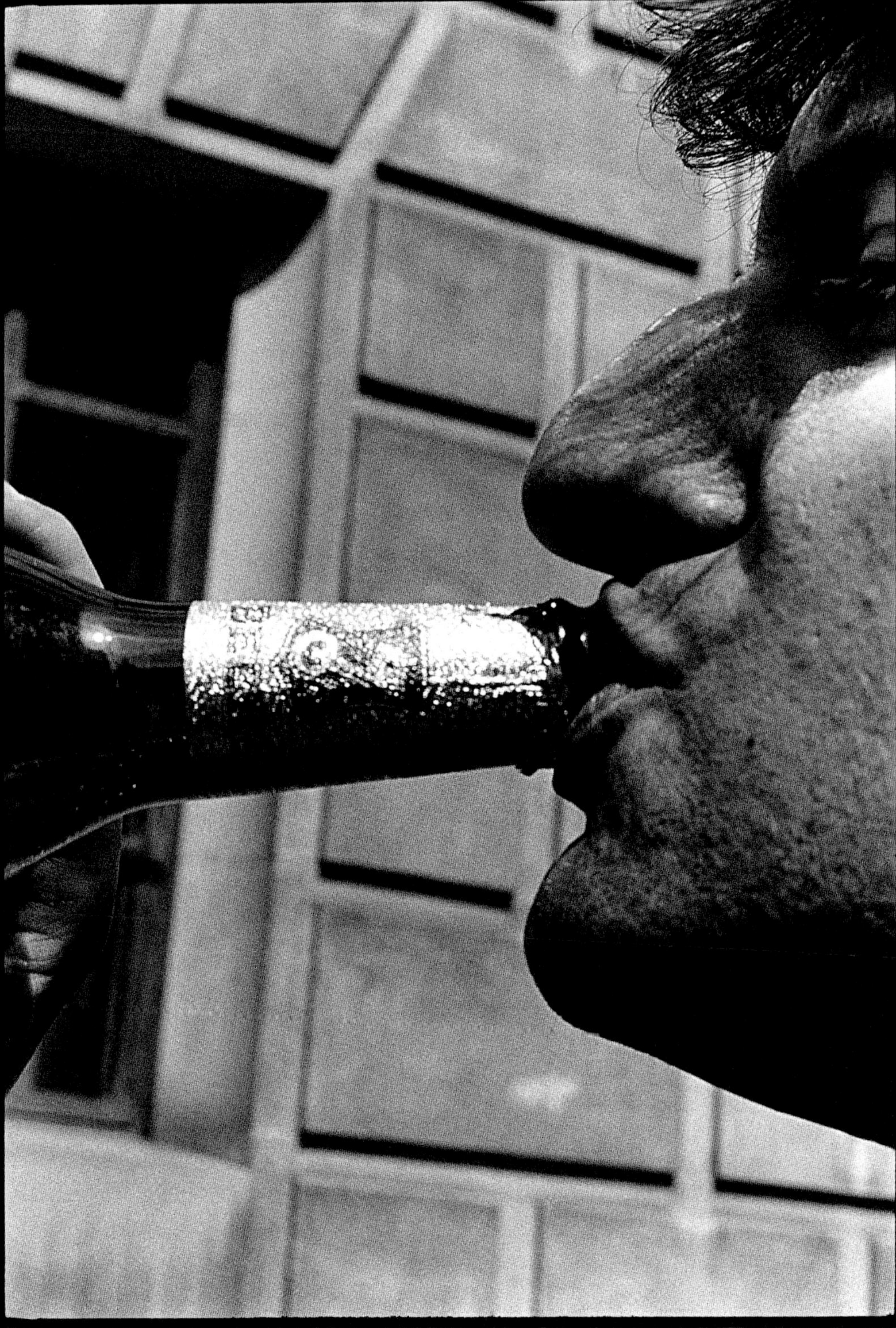

Brick Lane, 1982

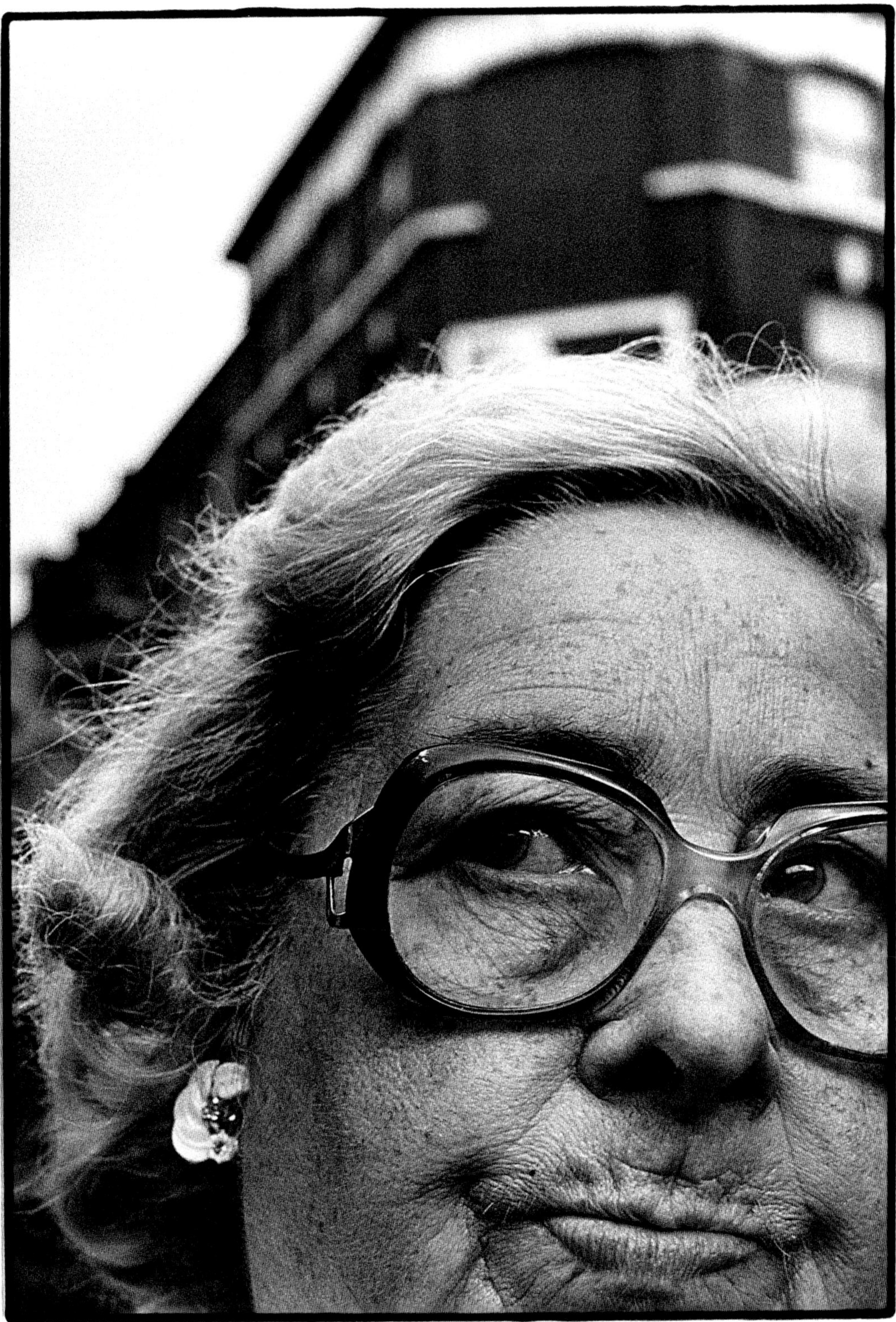

The City, 1989

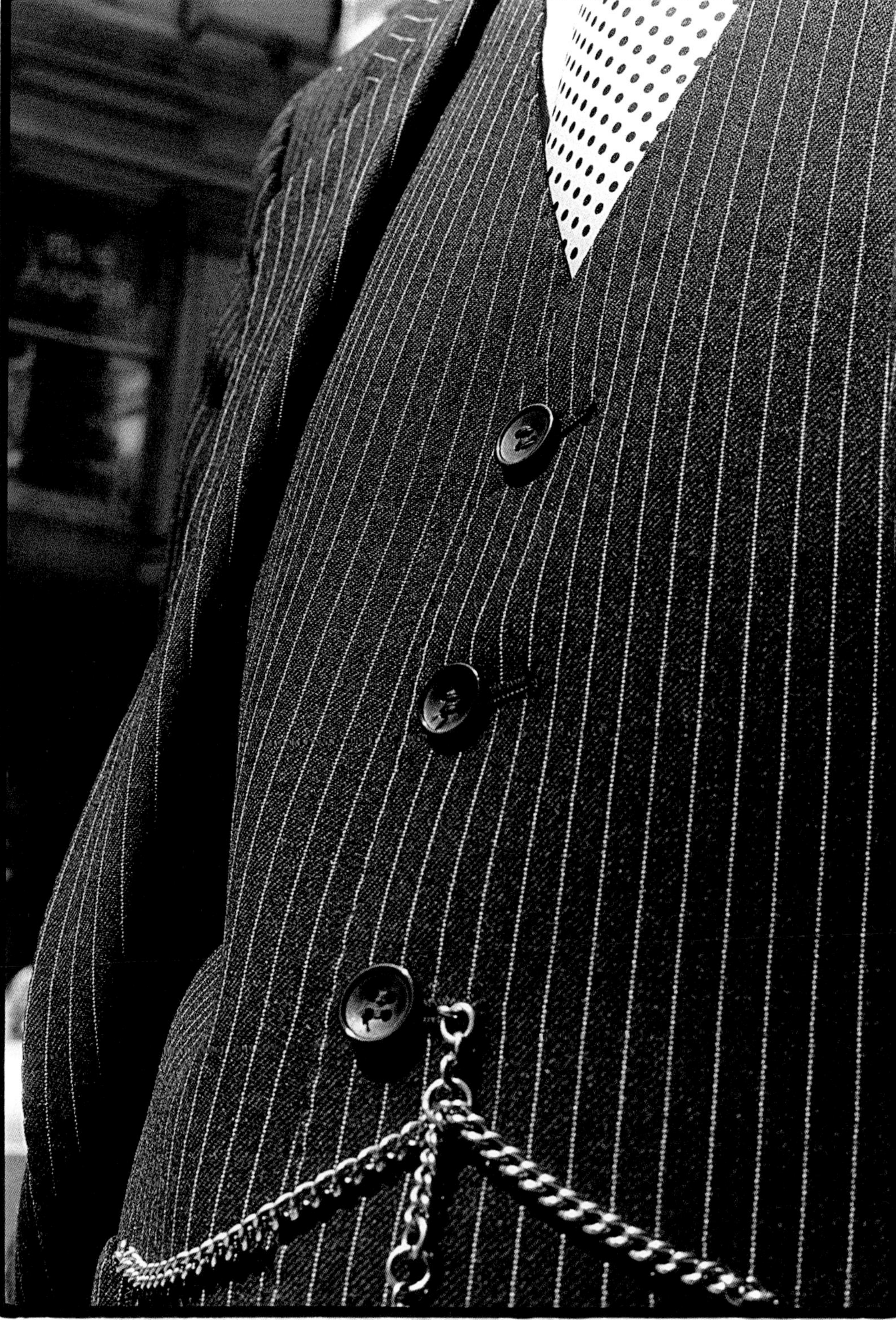

Brick Lane, 1982

Overleaf: The City, 1989

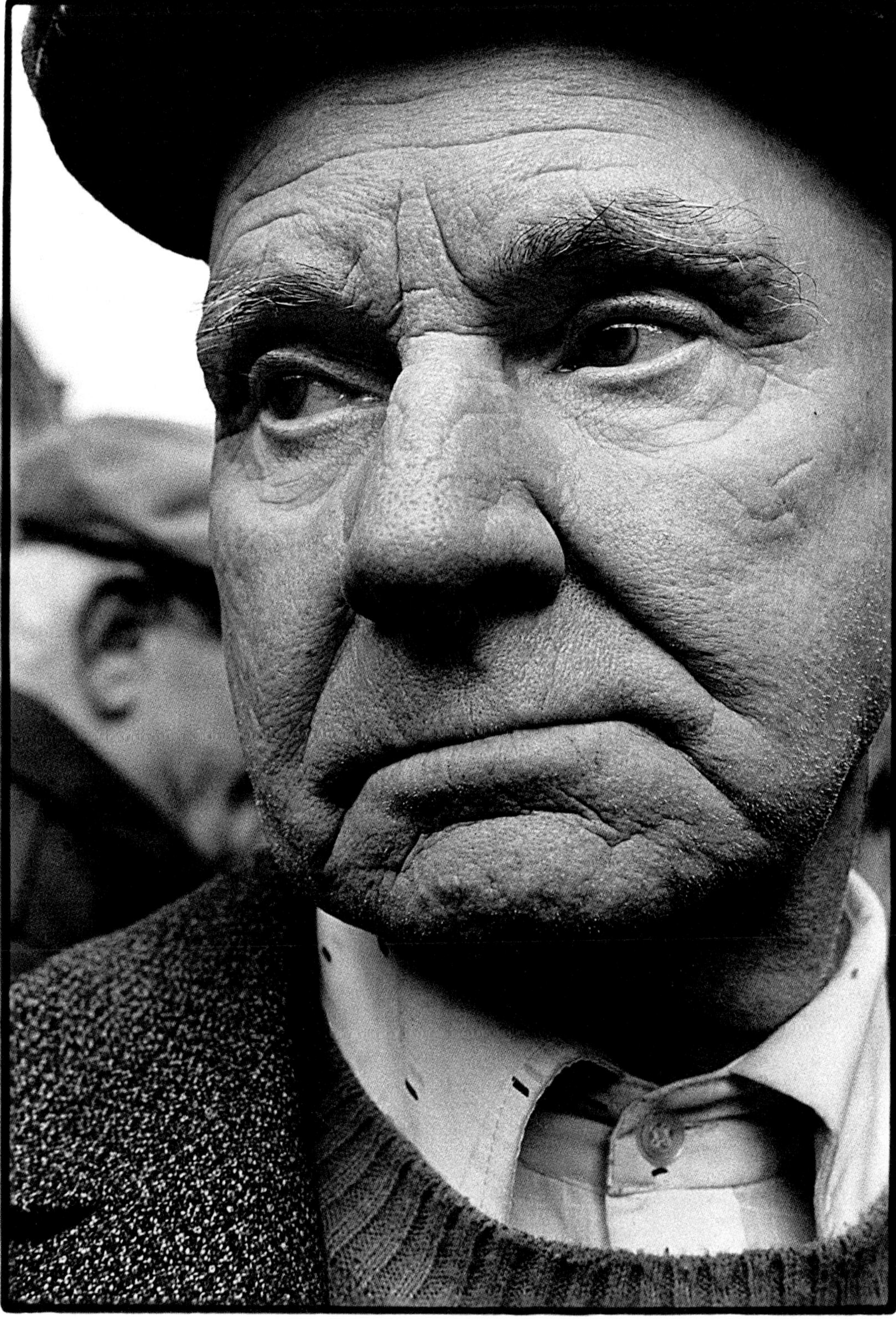

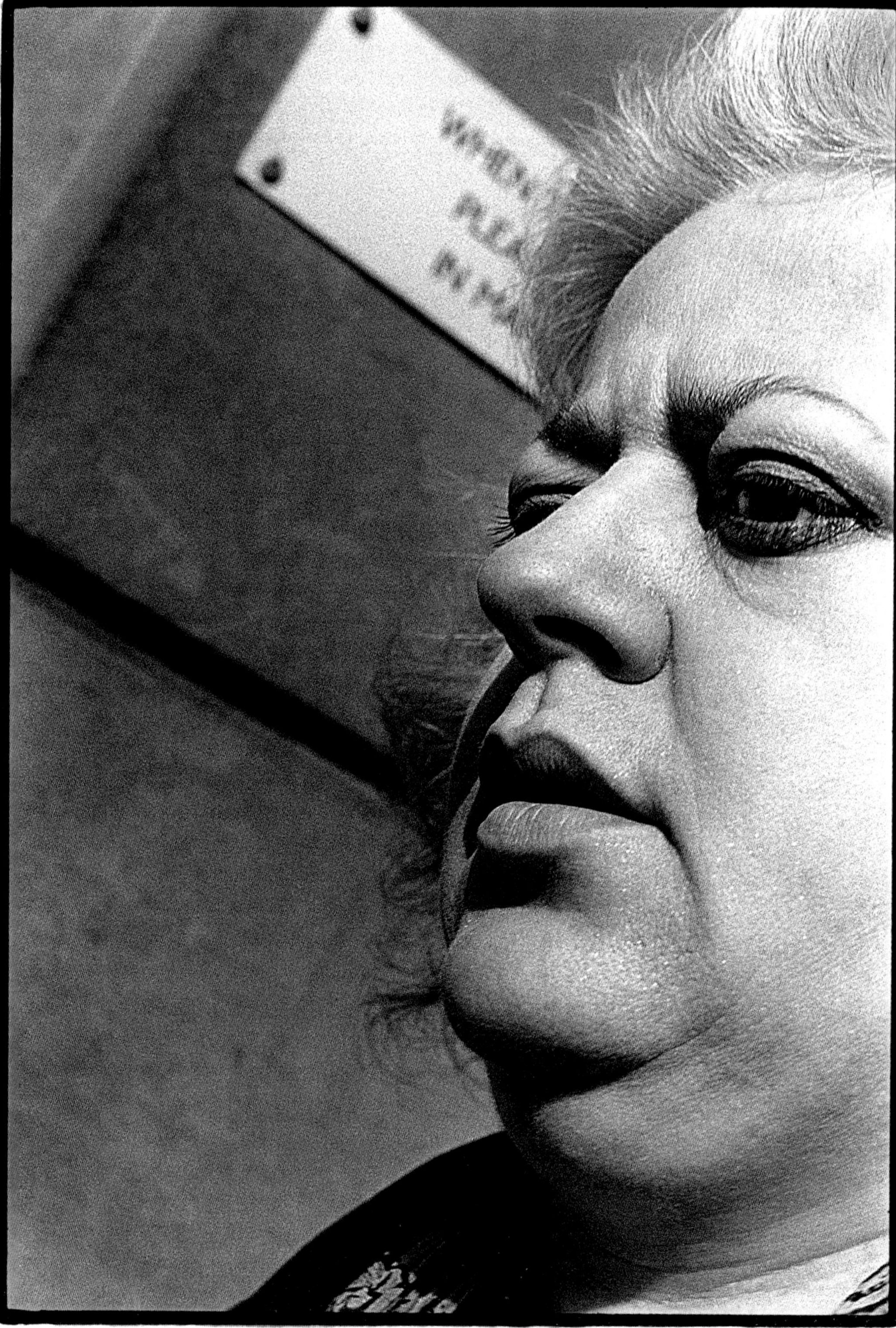

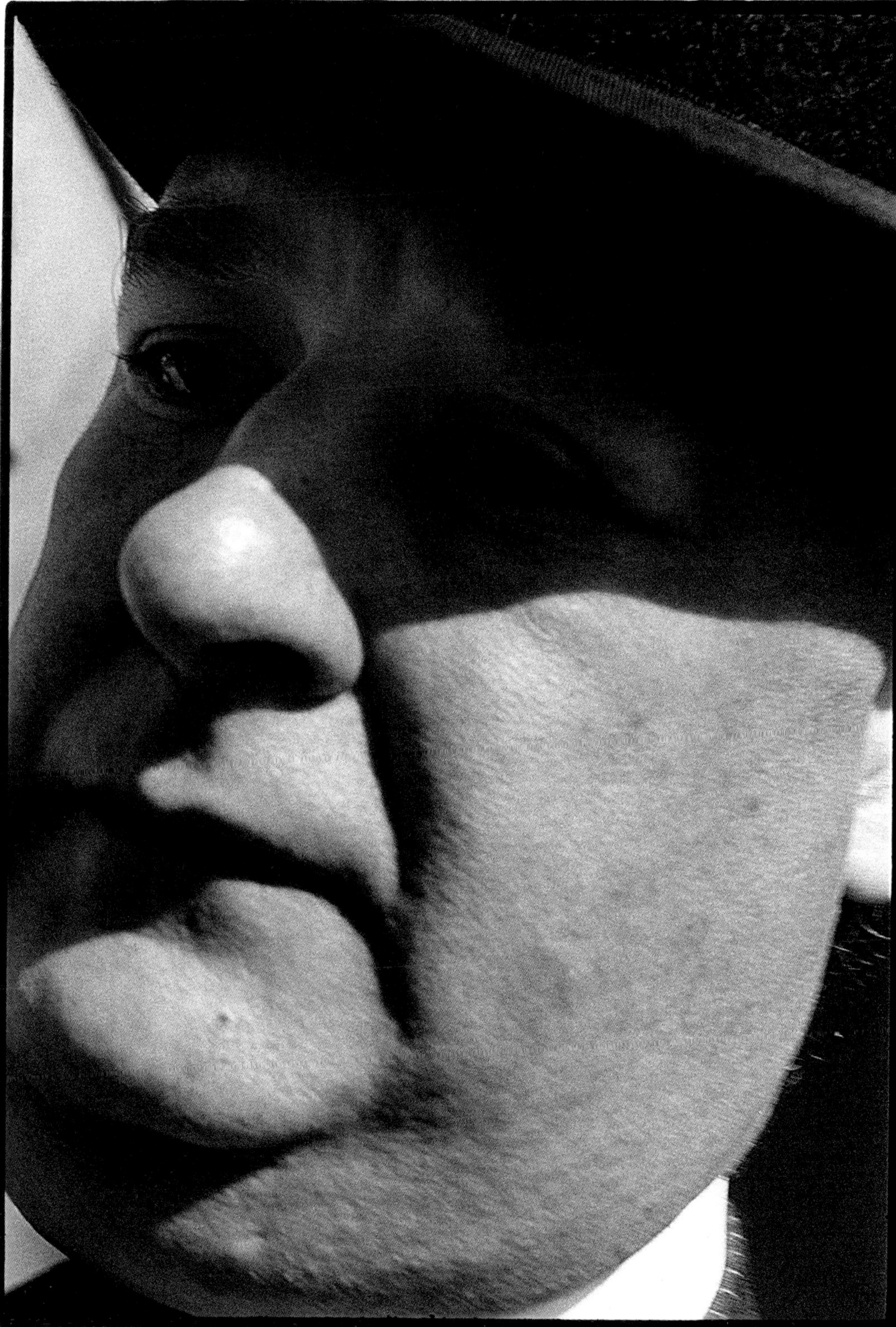

Brick Lane, 1989

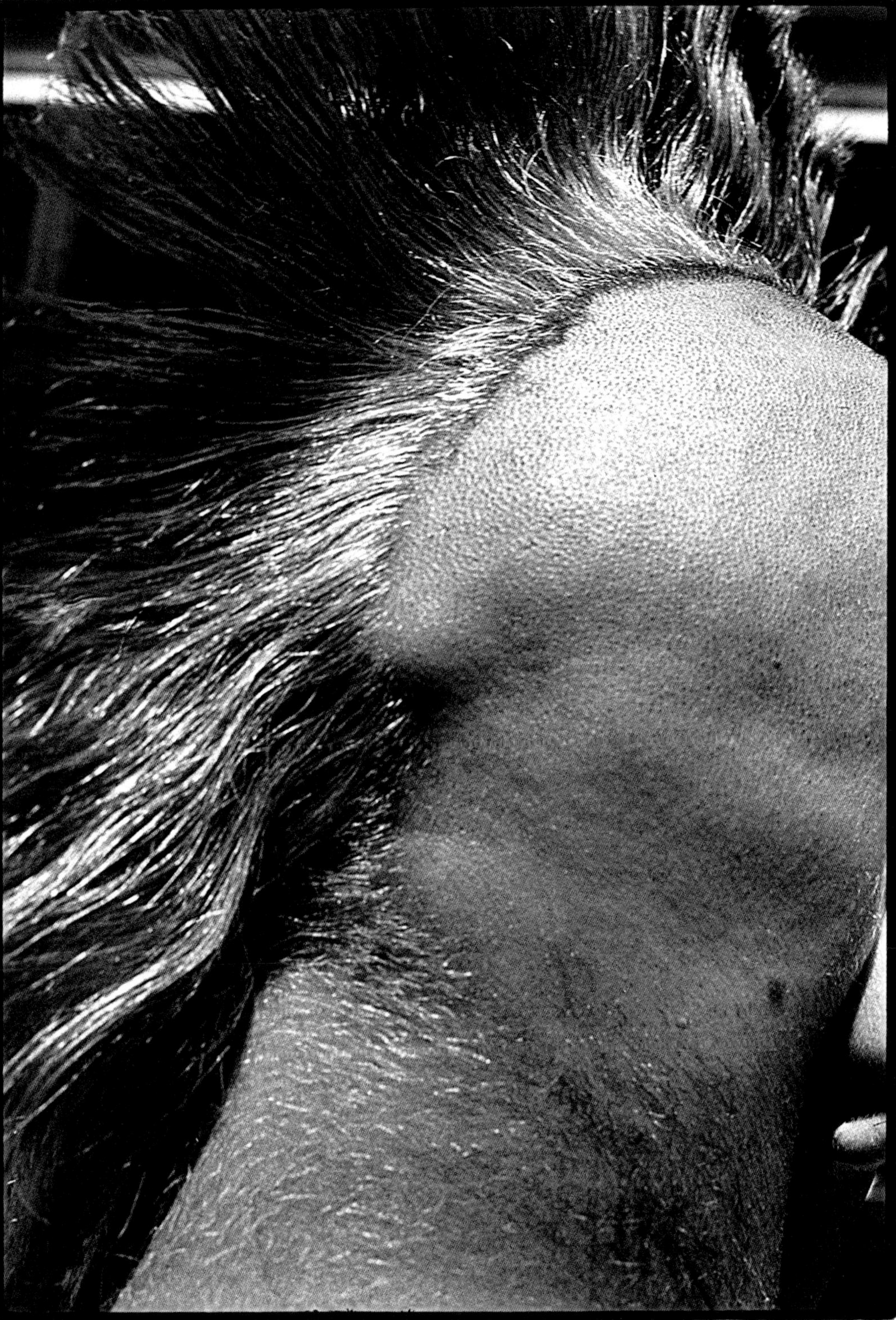

The City, 1989

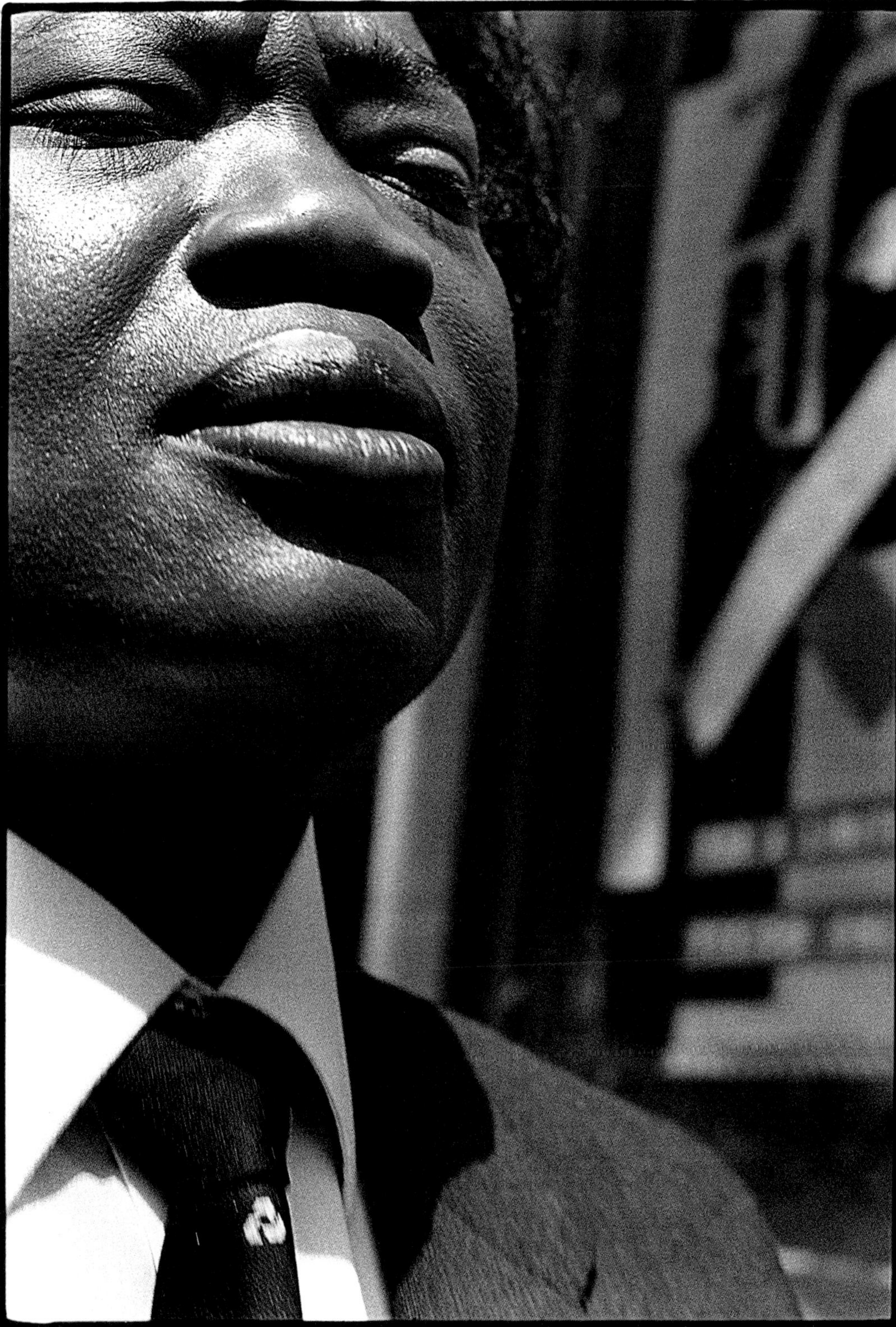

Brick Lane, 1989

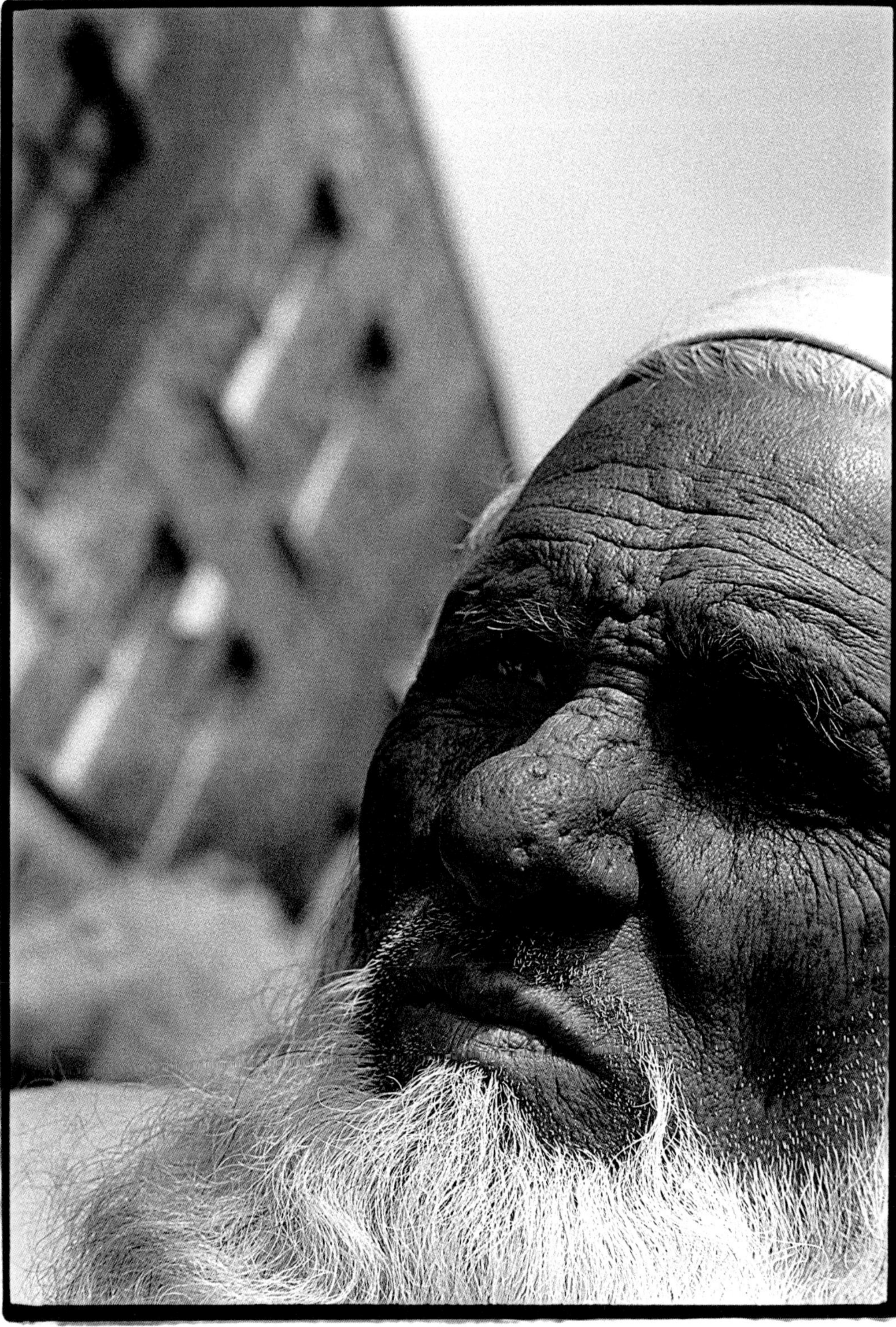

The City, 1992

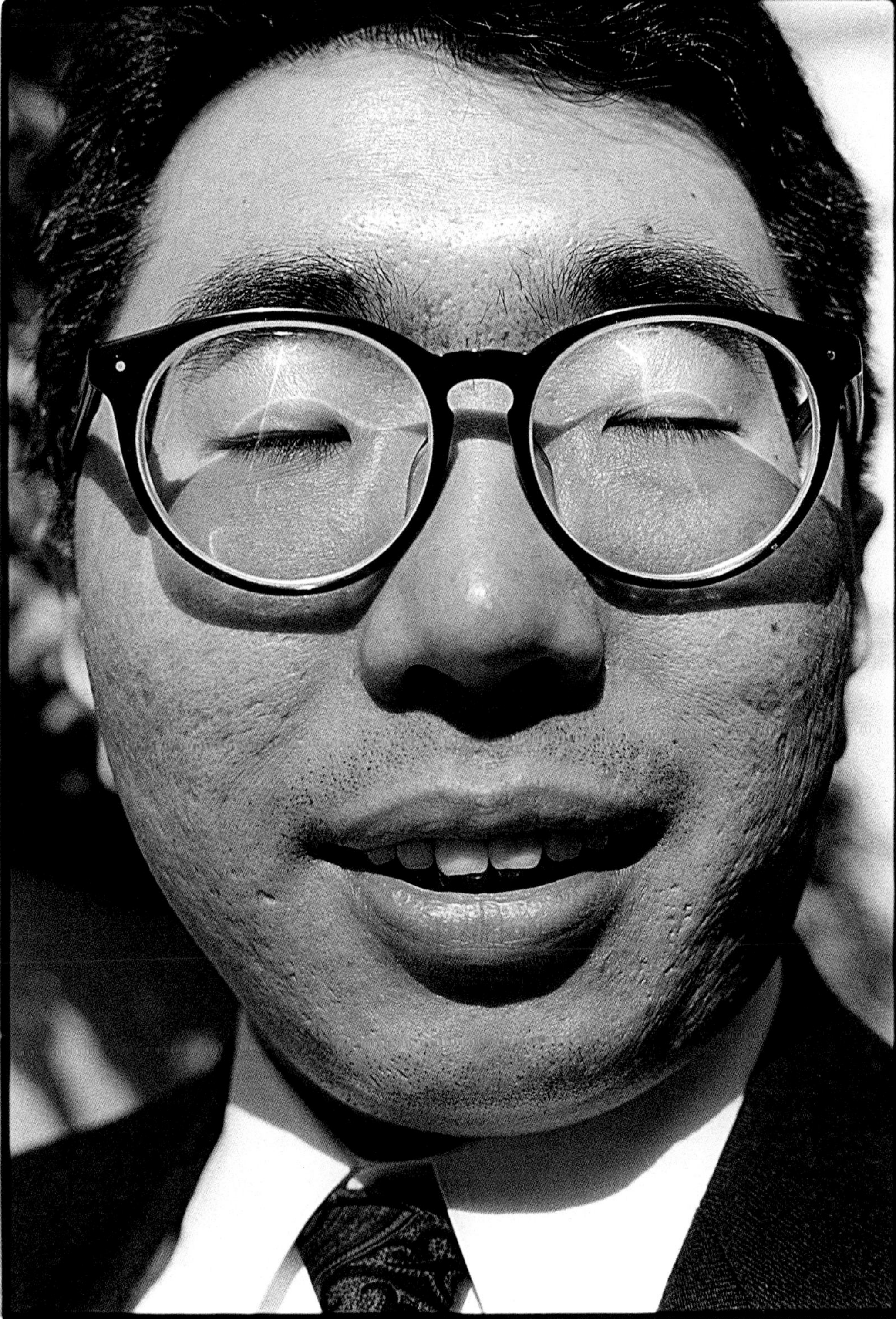

Brick Lane, 1982

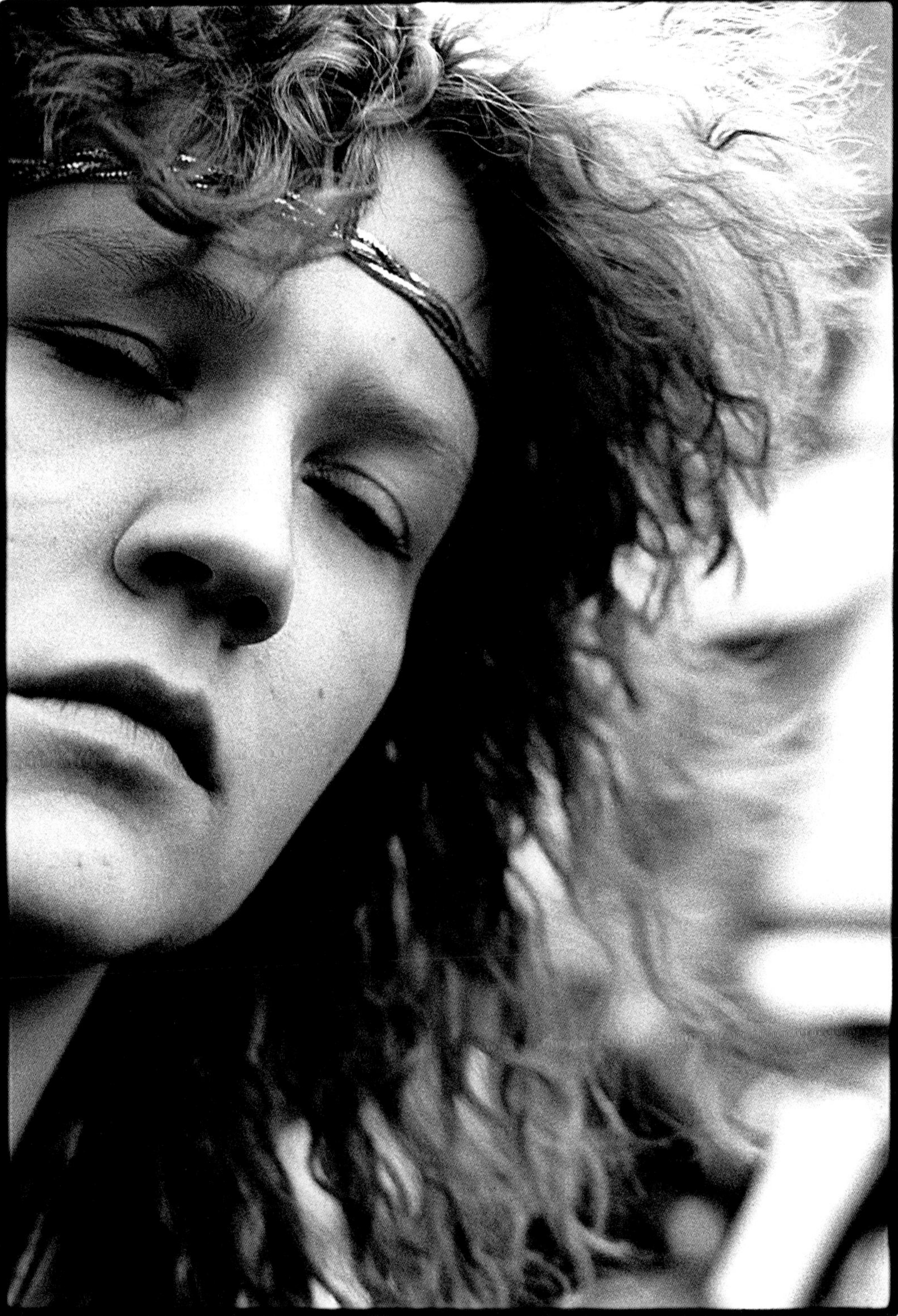

The City, 1989

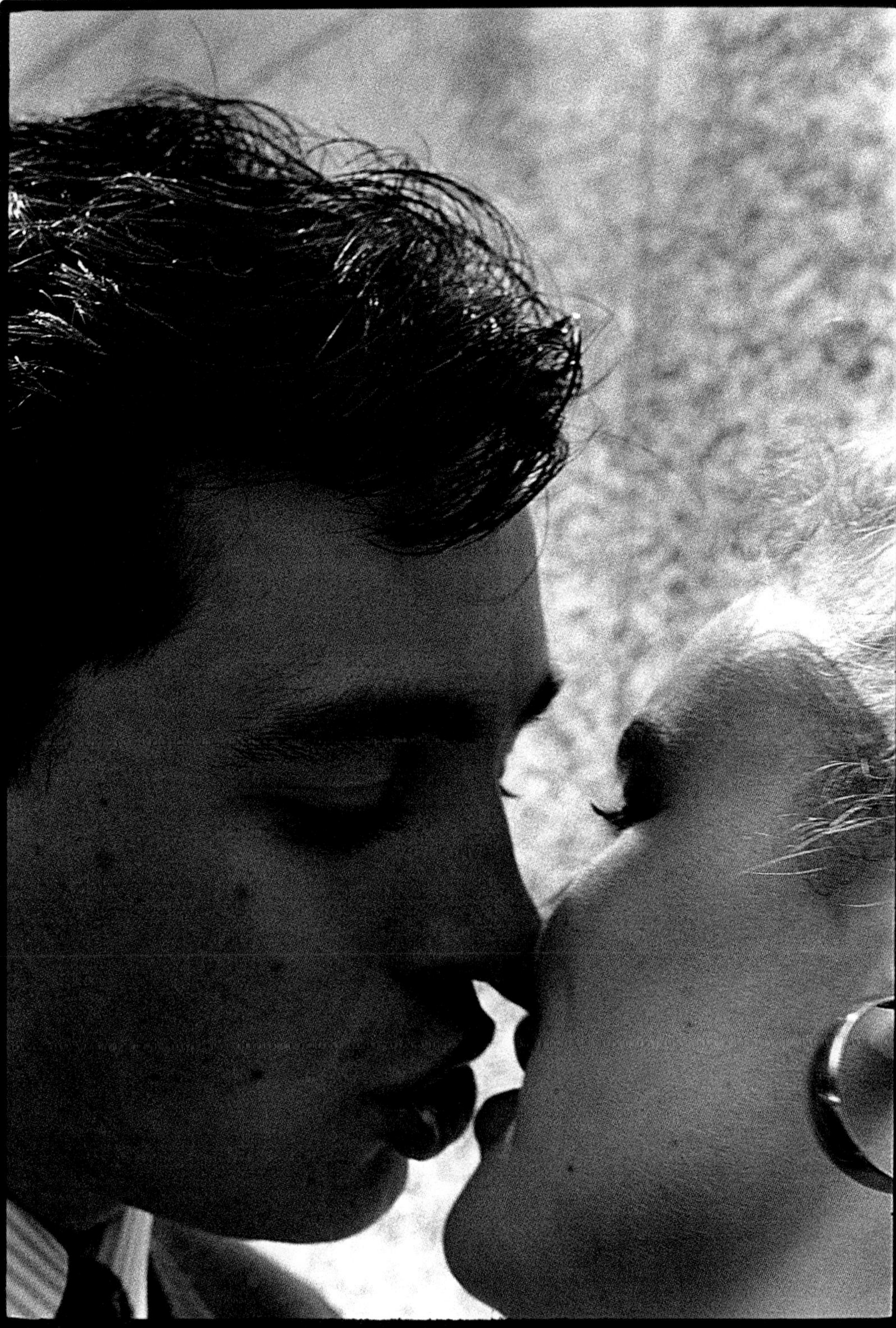

Brick Lane, 1977

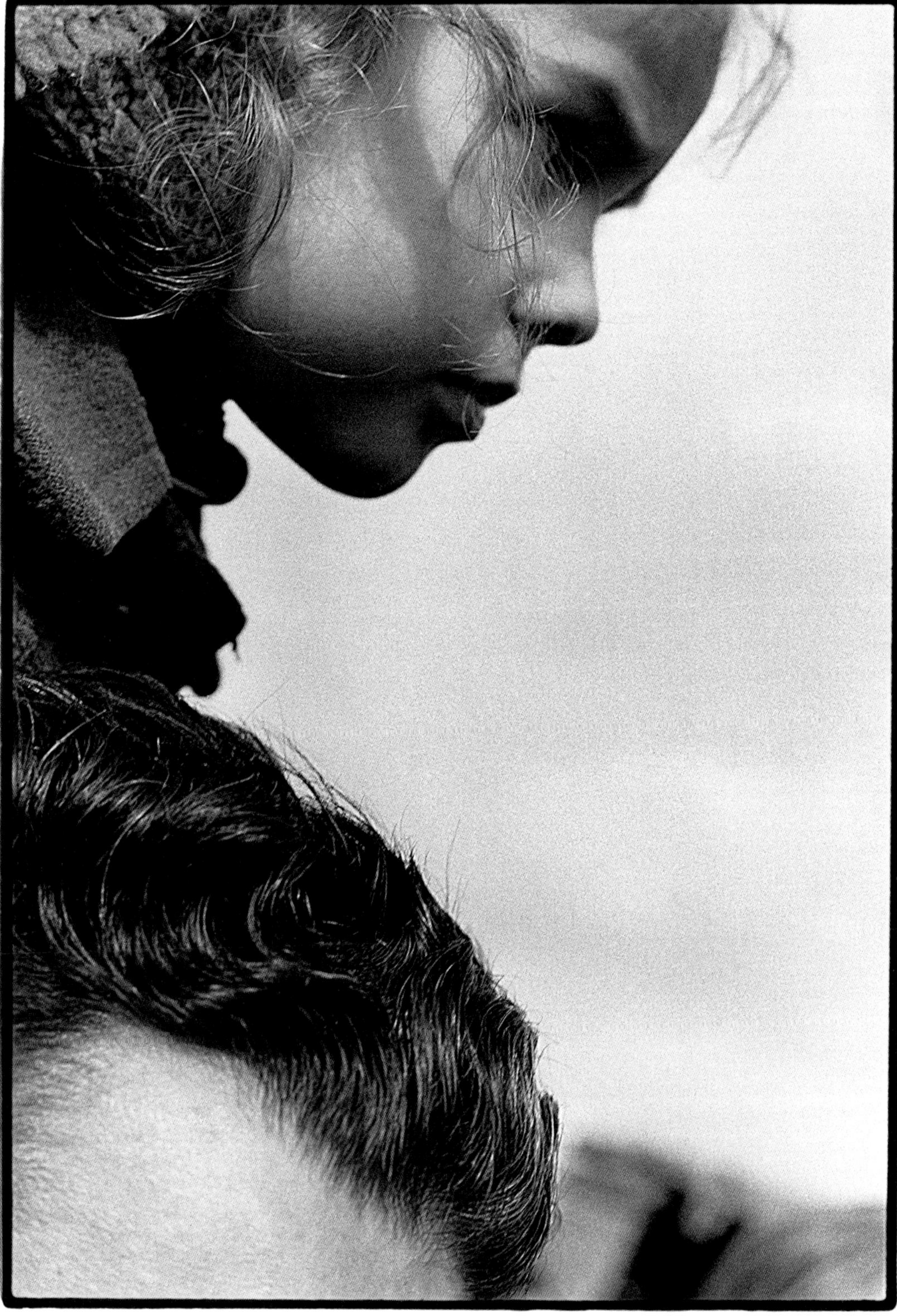

The City, 1989

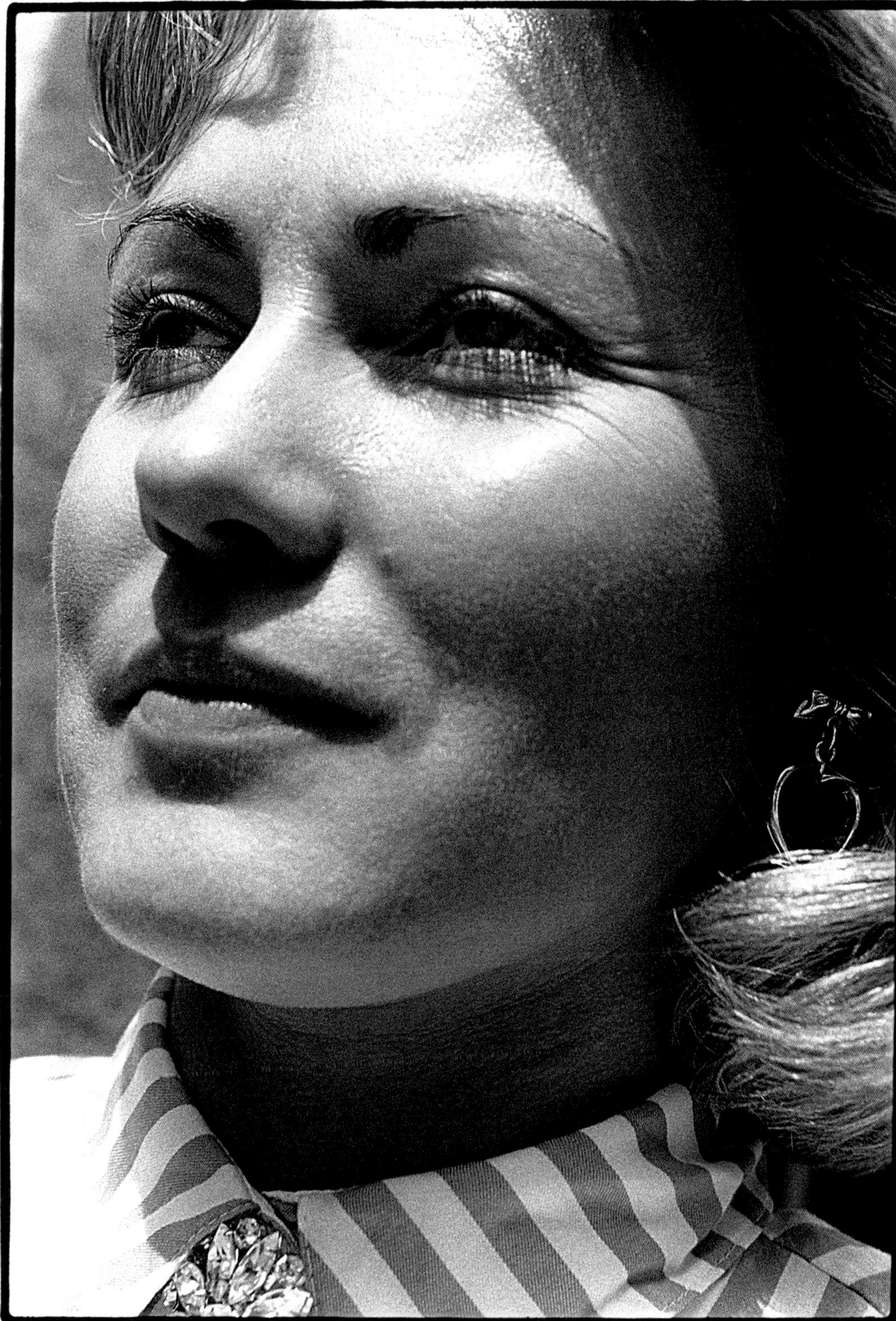

Brick Lane, 1983

Overleaf: The City, 1989

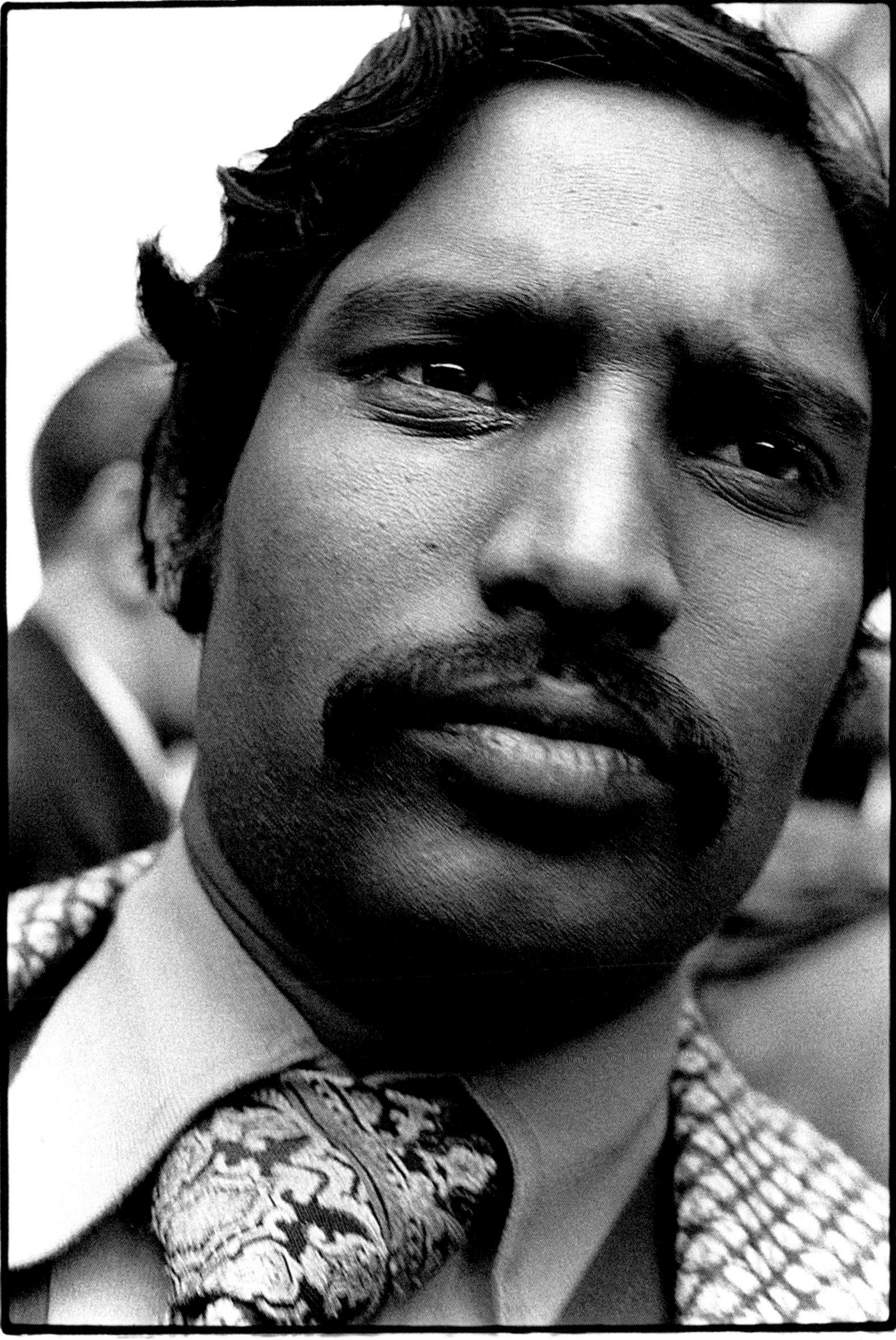

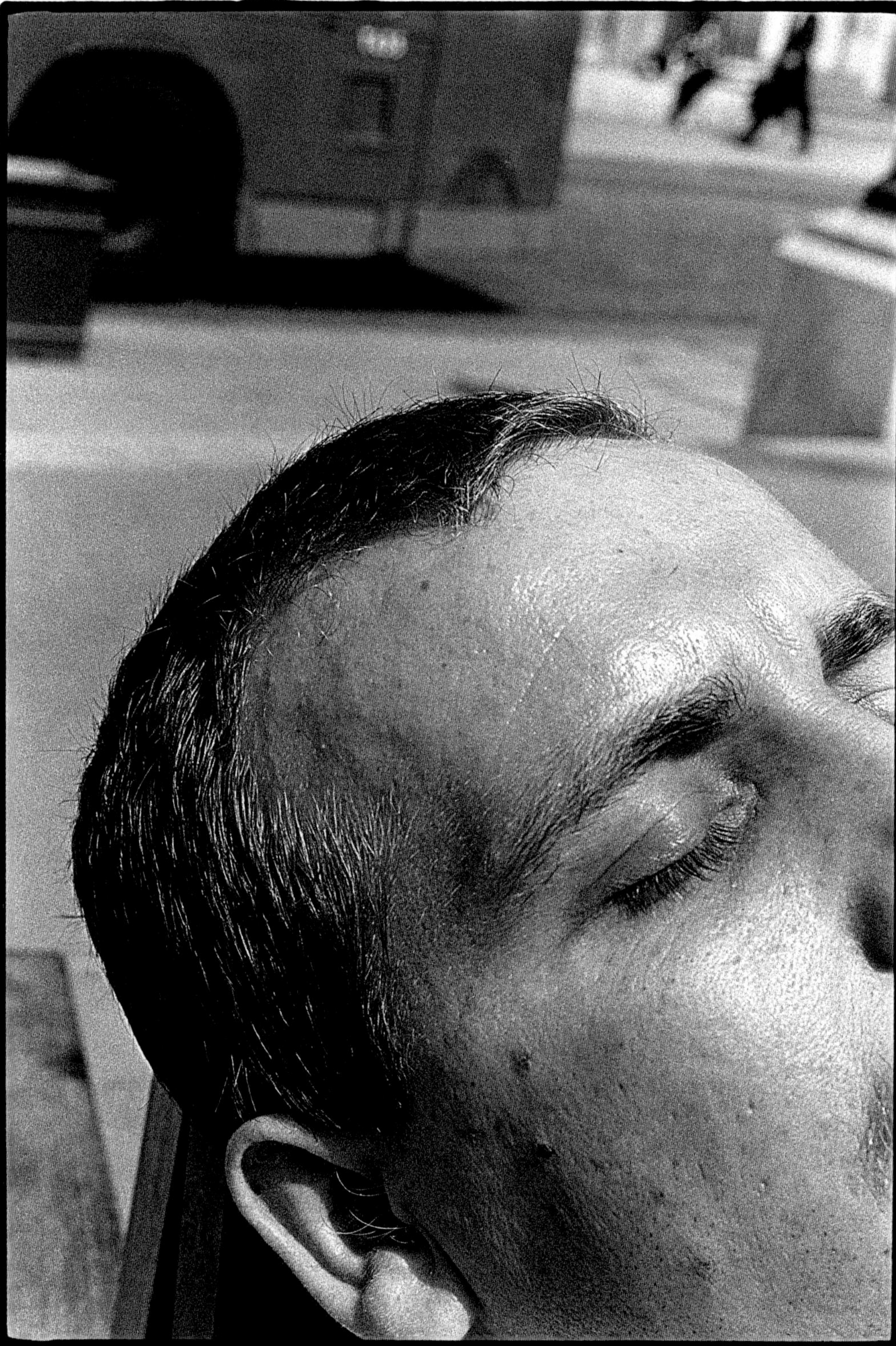

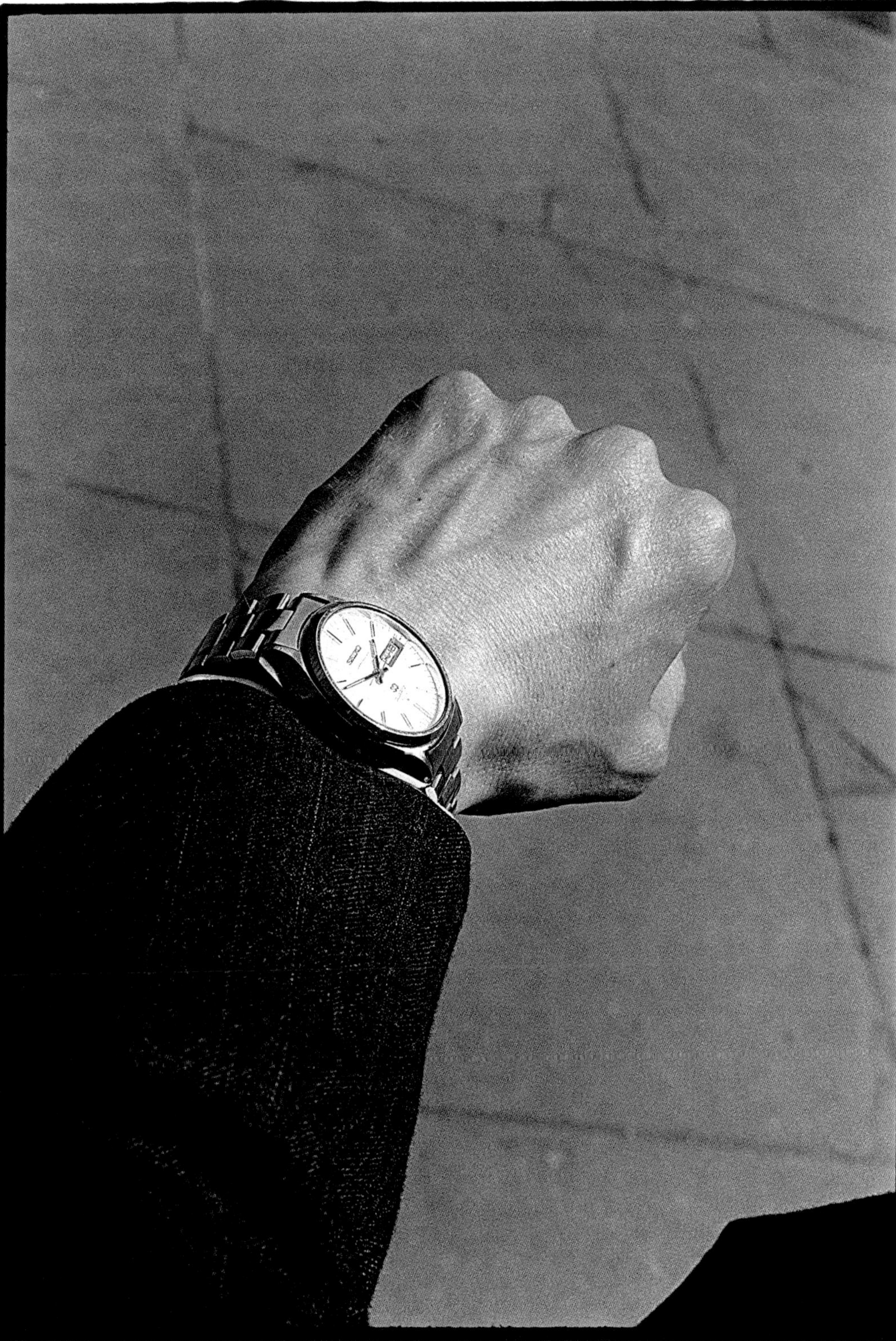

Brick Lane, 1991

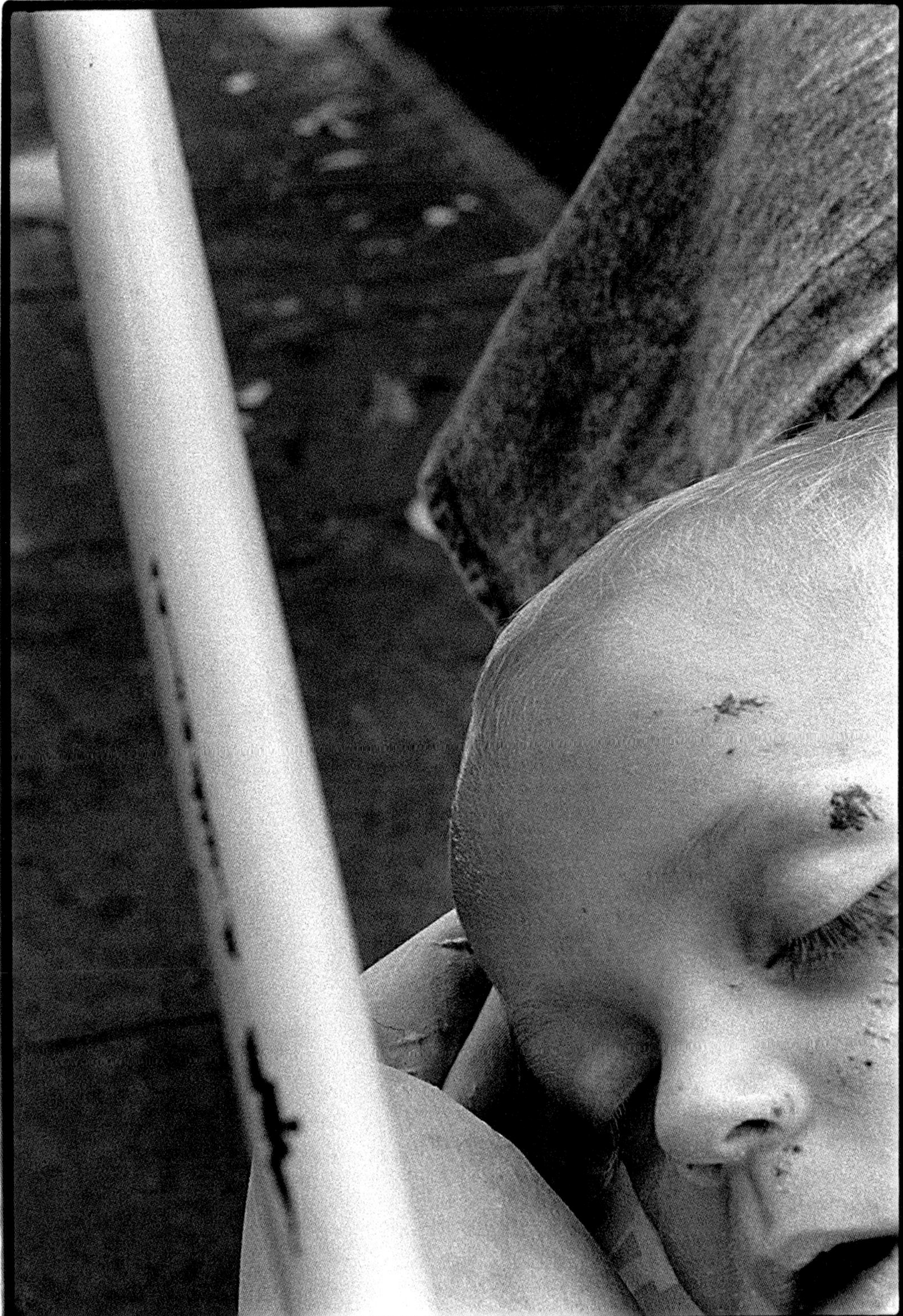

The City, 1989

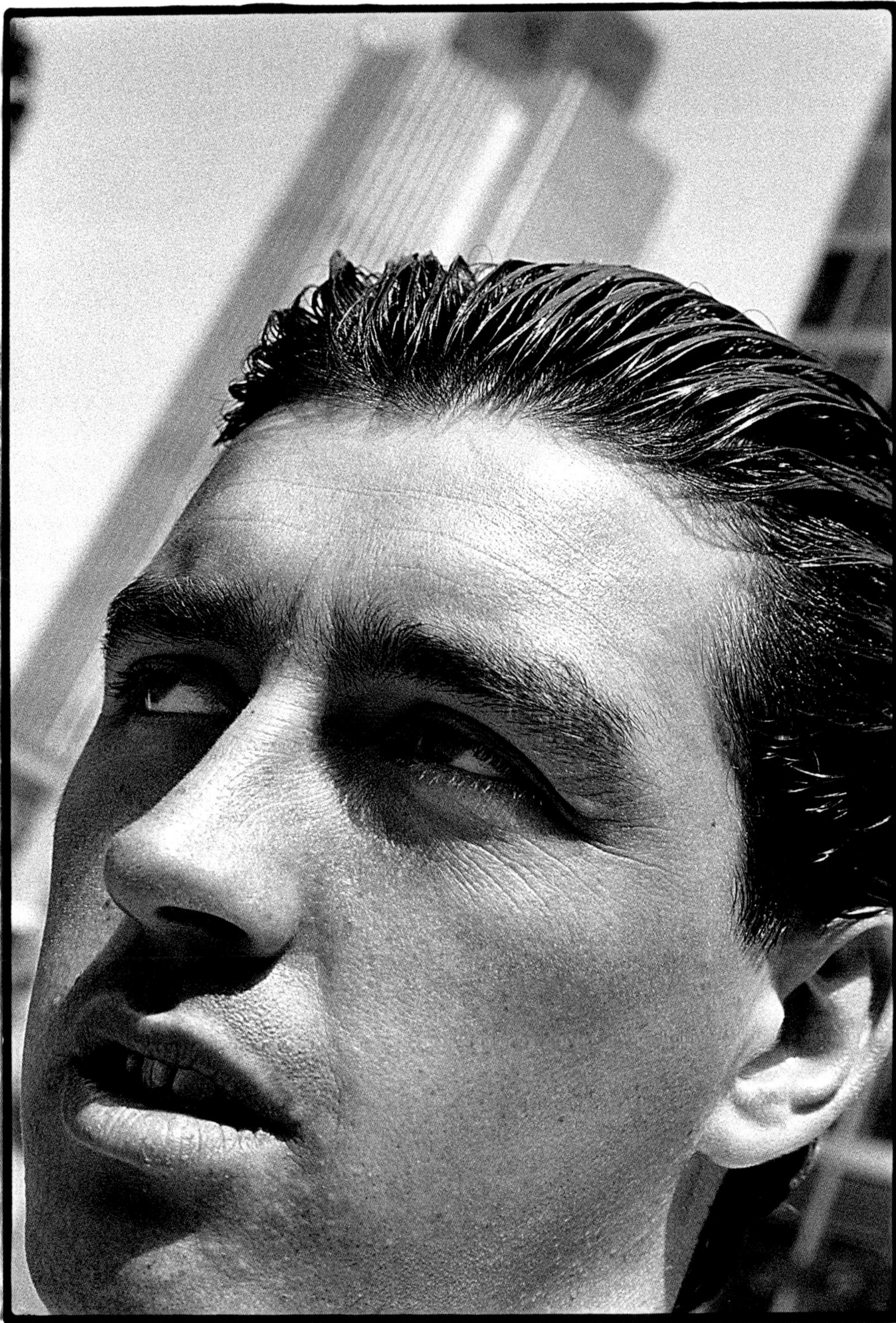

Brick Lane, 1982

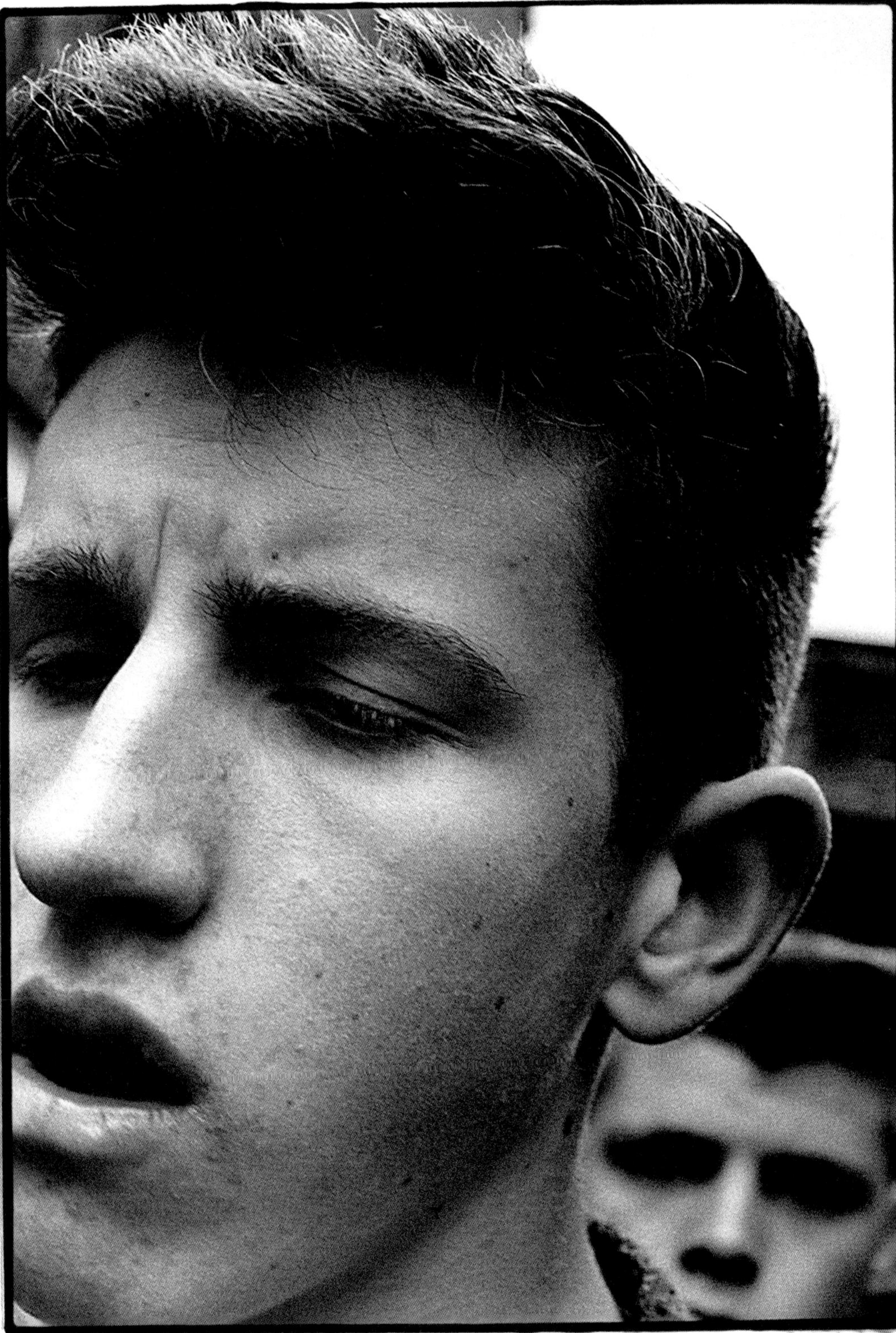

The City, 1992

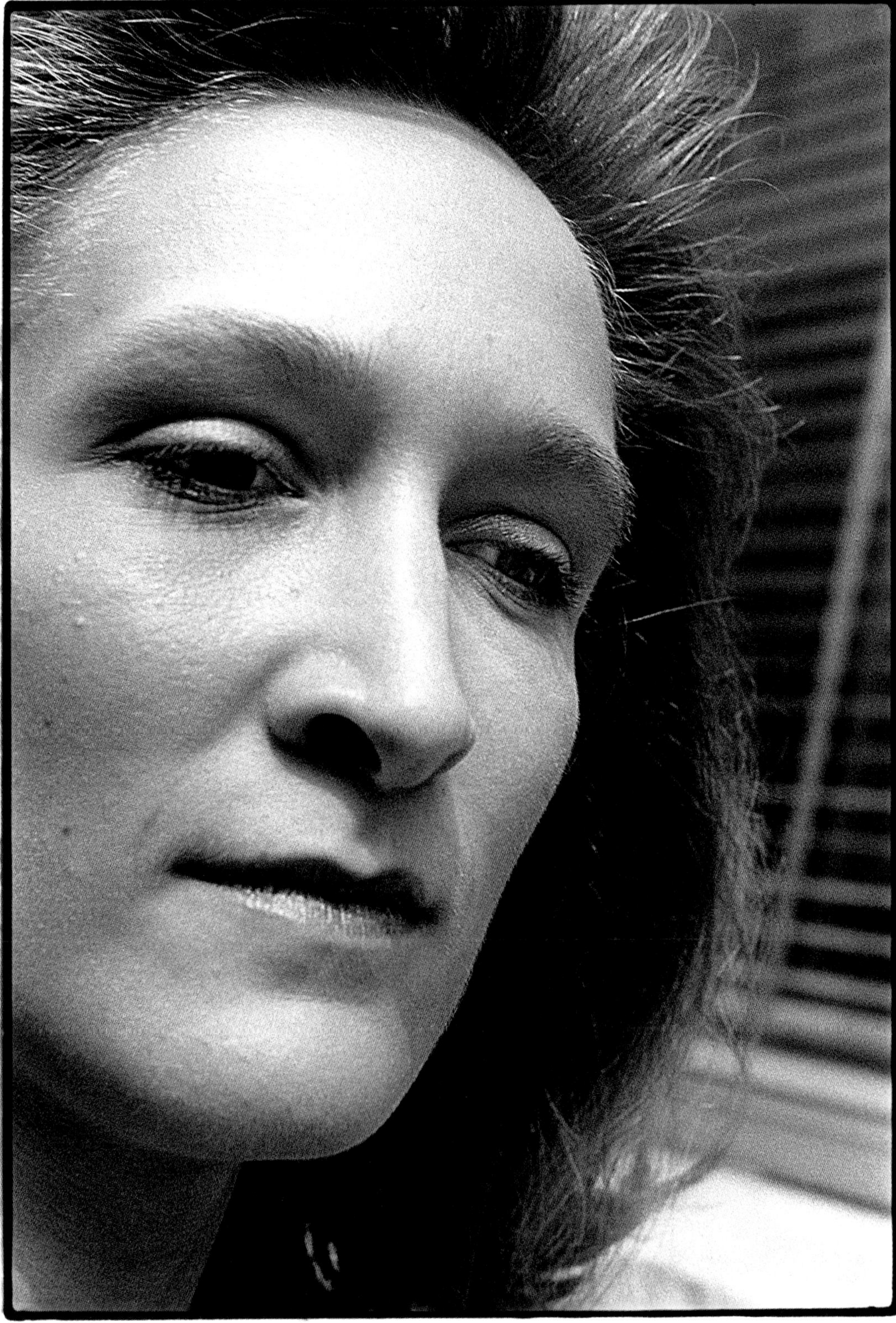

Brick Lane, 1977

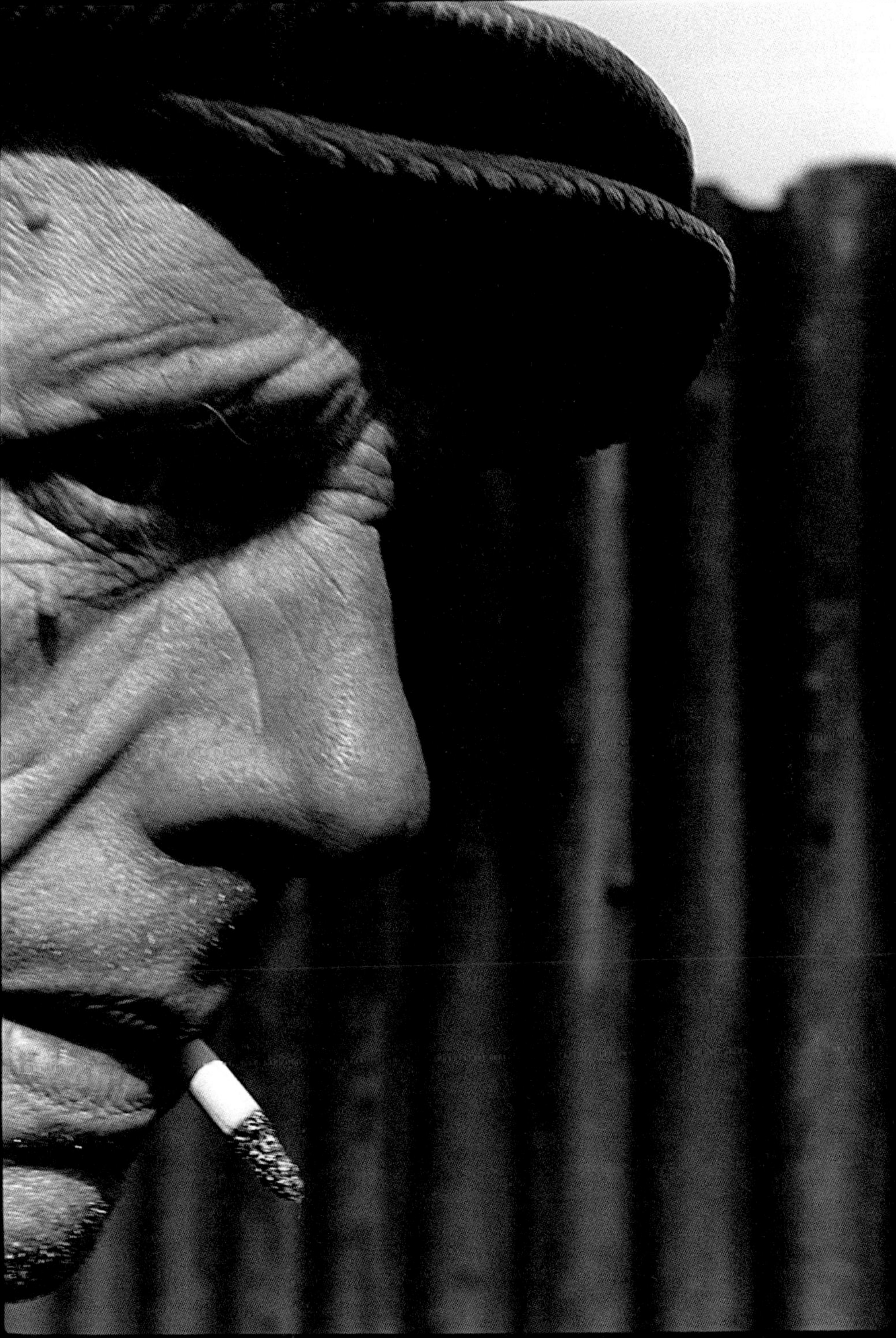

The City, 1989

Overleaf: Brick Lane, 1991

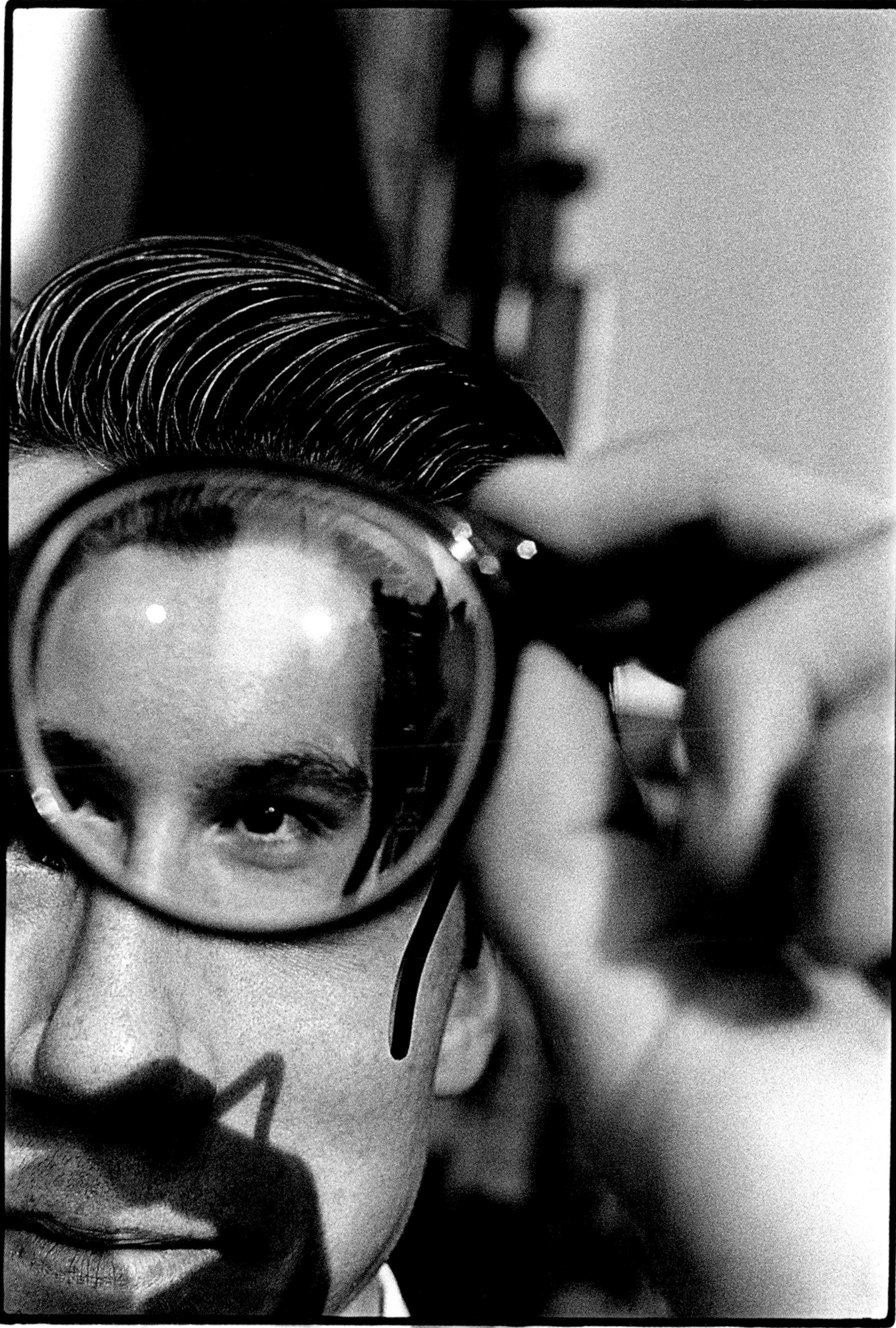

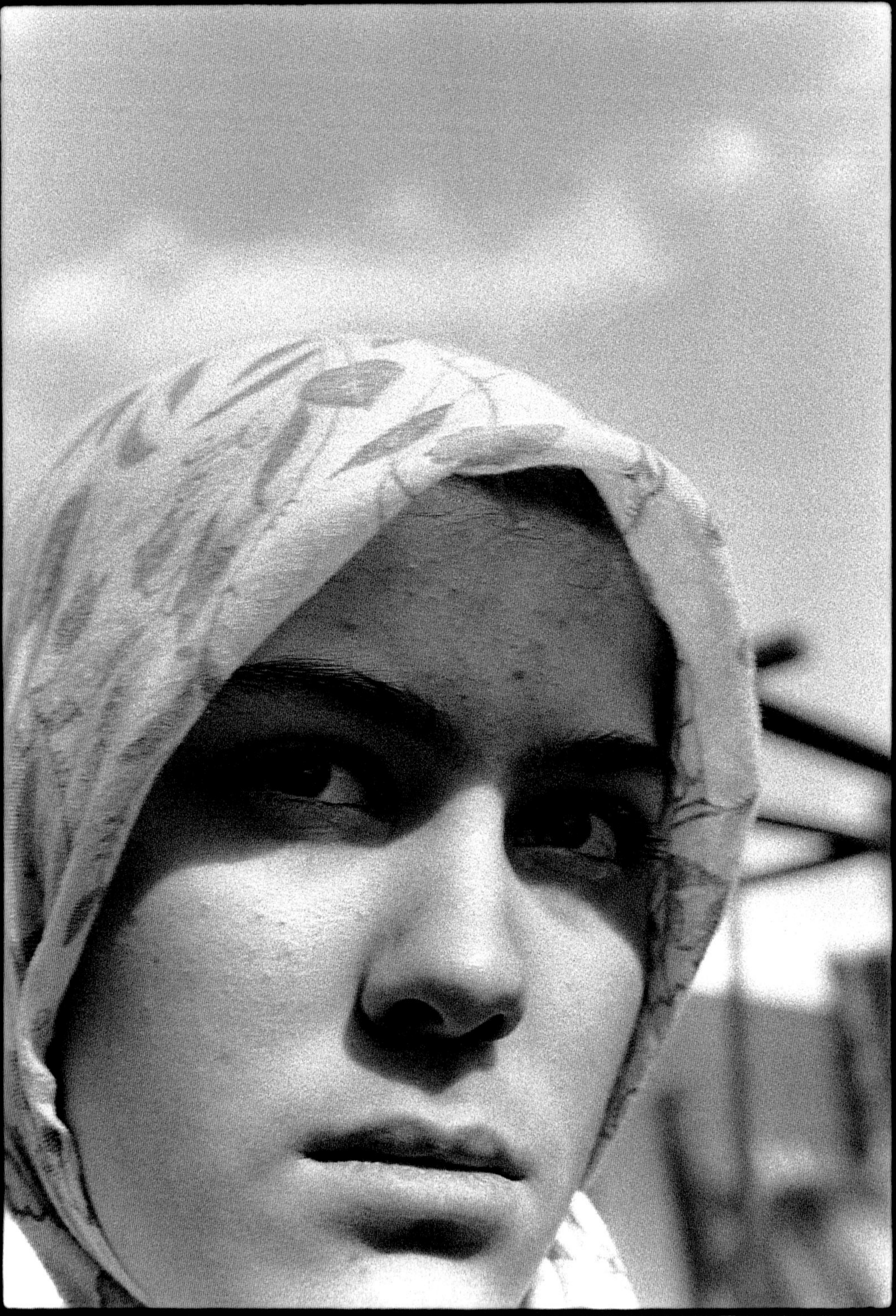

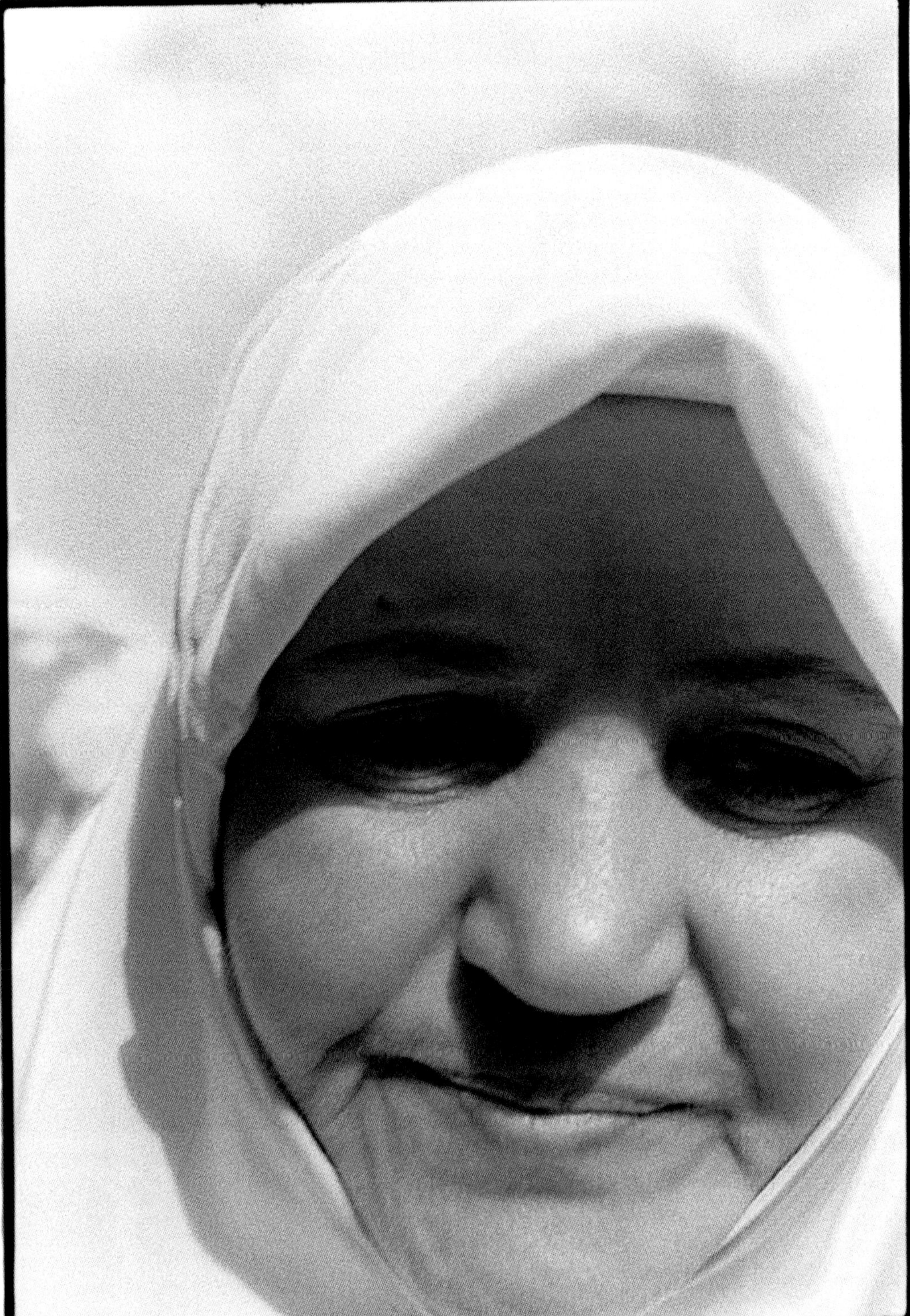

The City, 1989

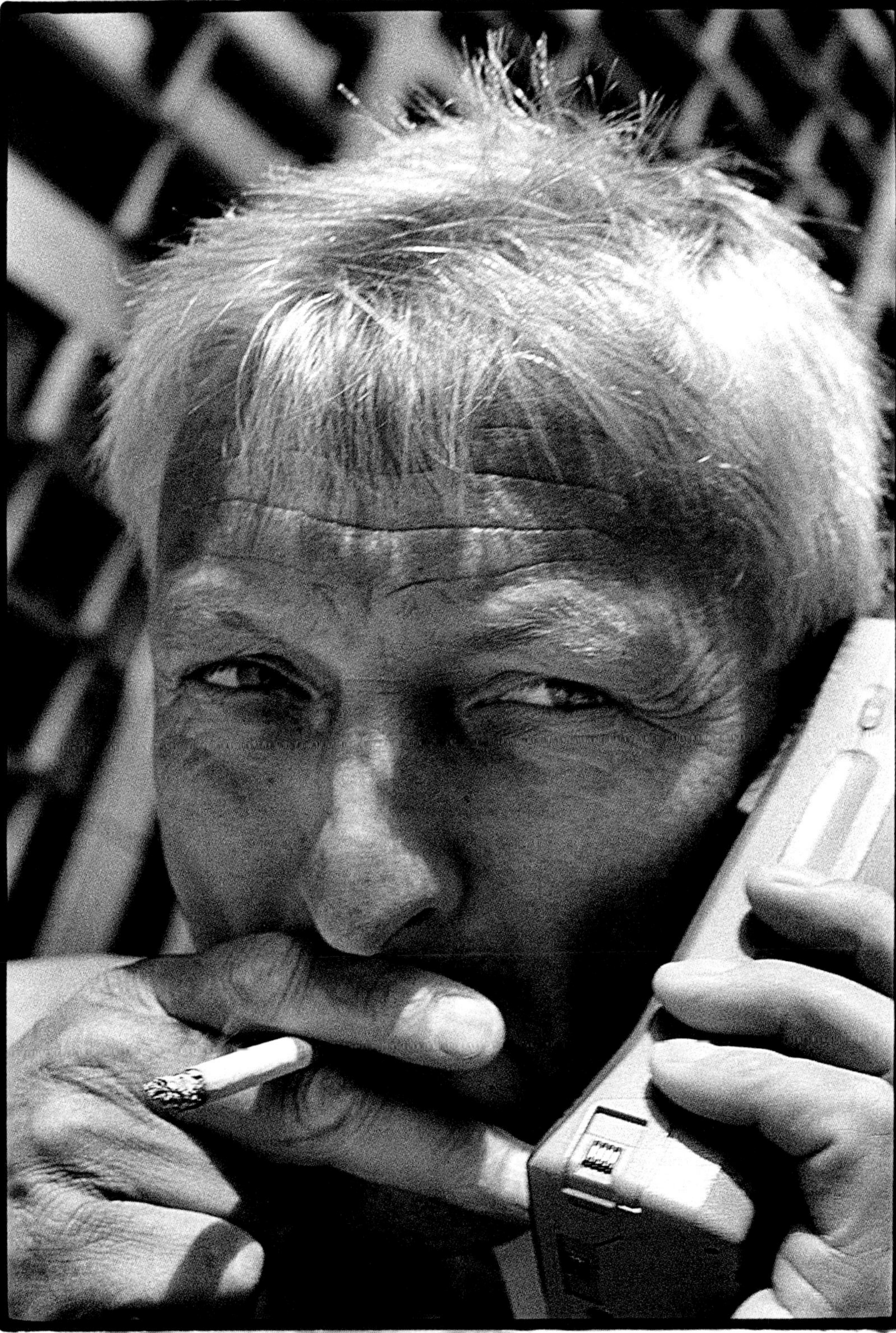

Brick Lane, 1989

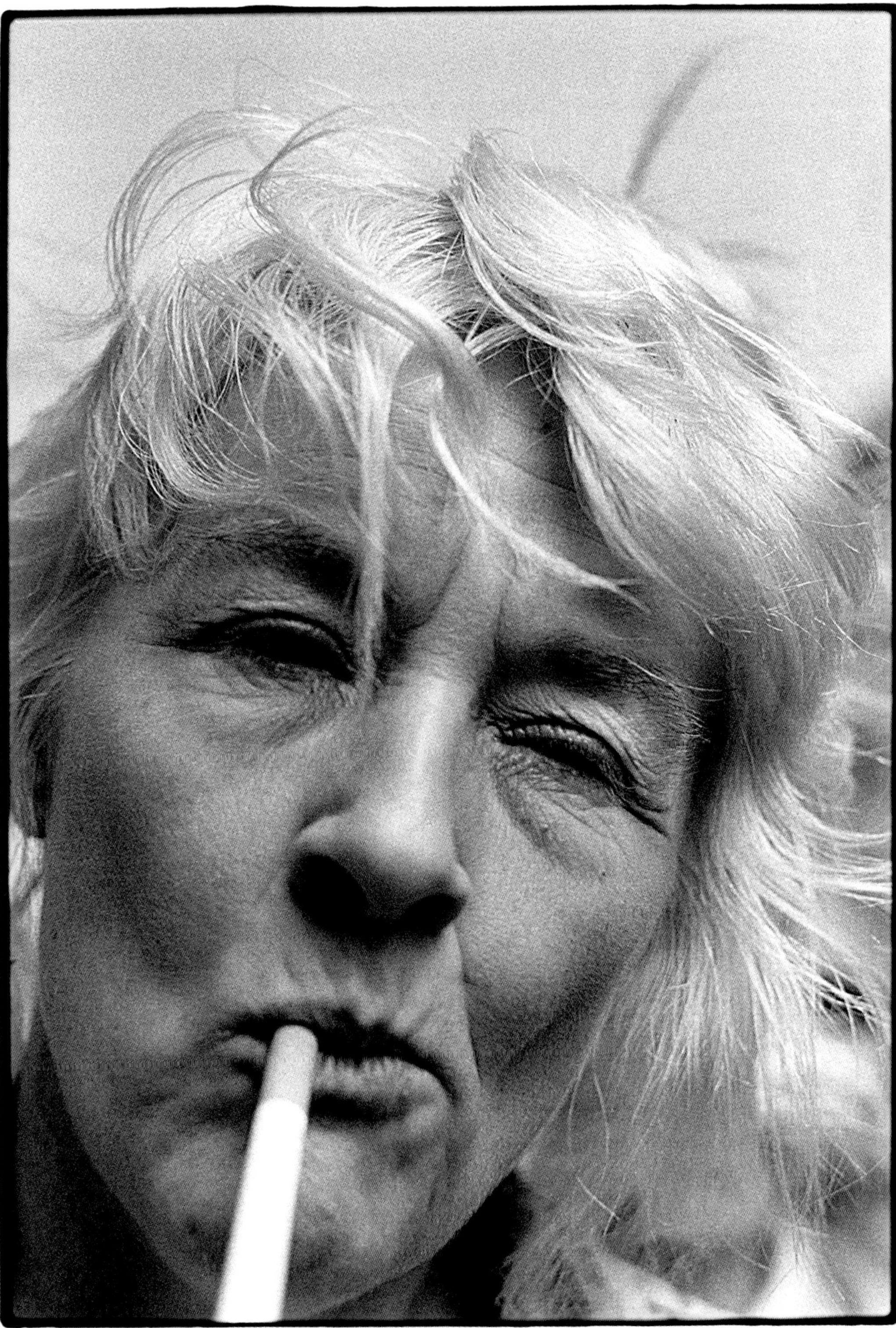

The City, 1989

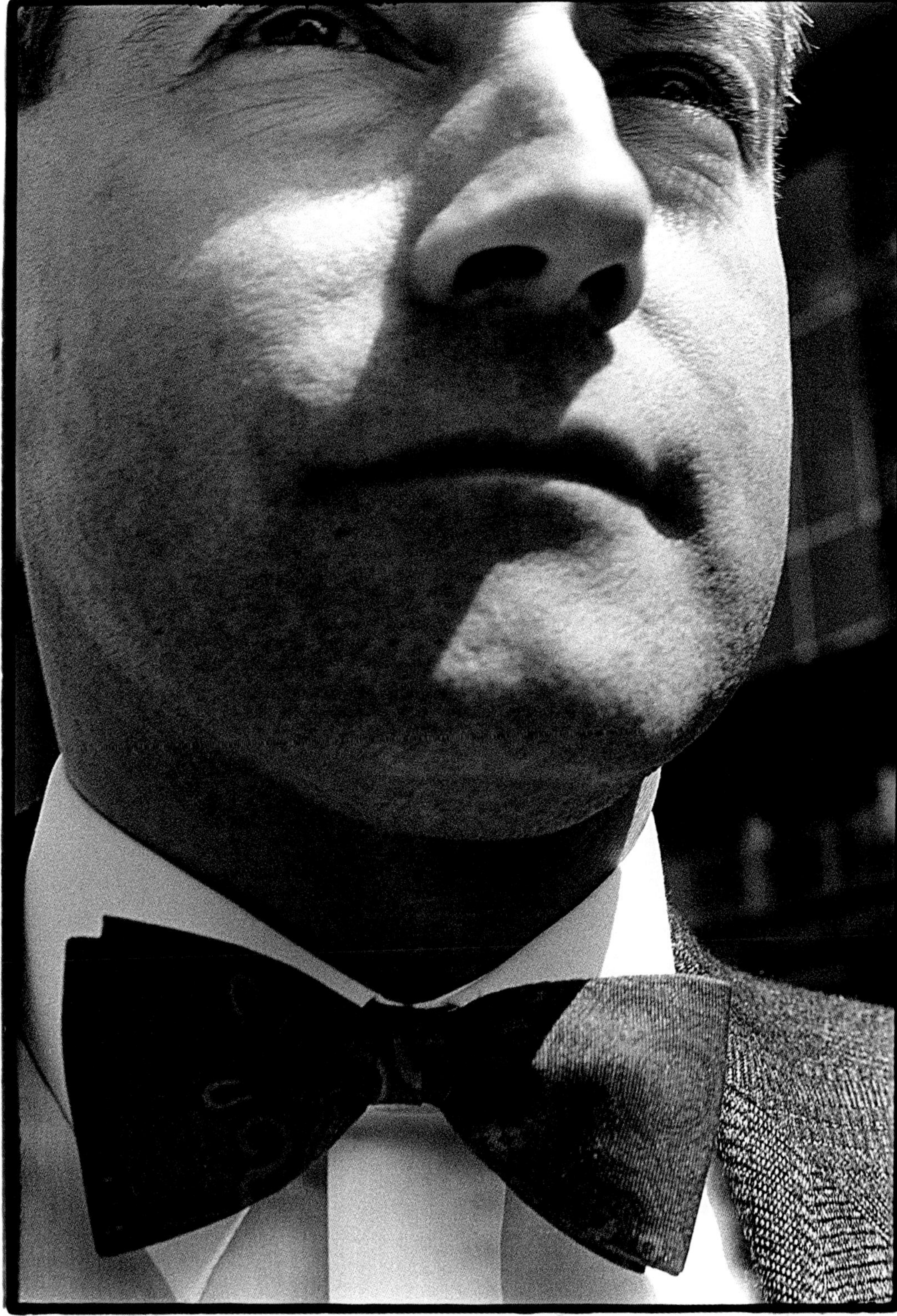

Brick Lane, 1992

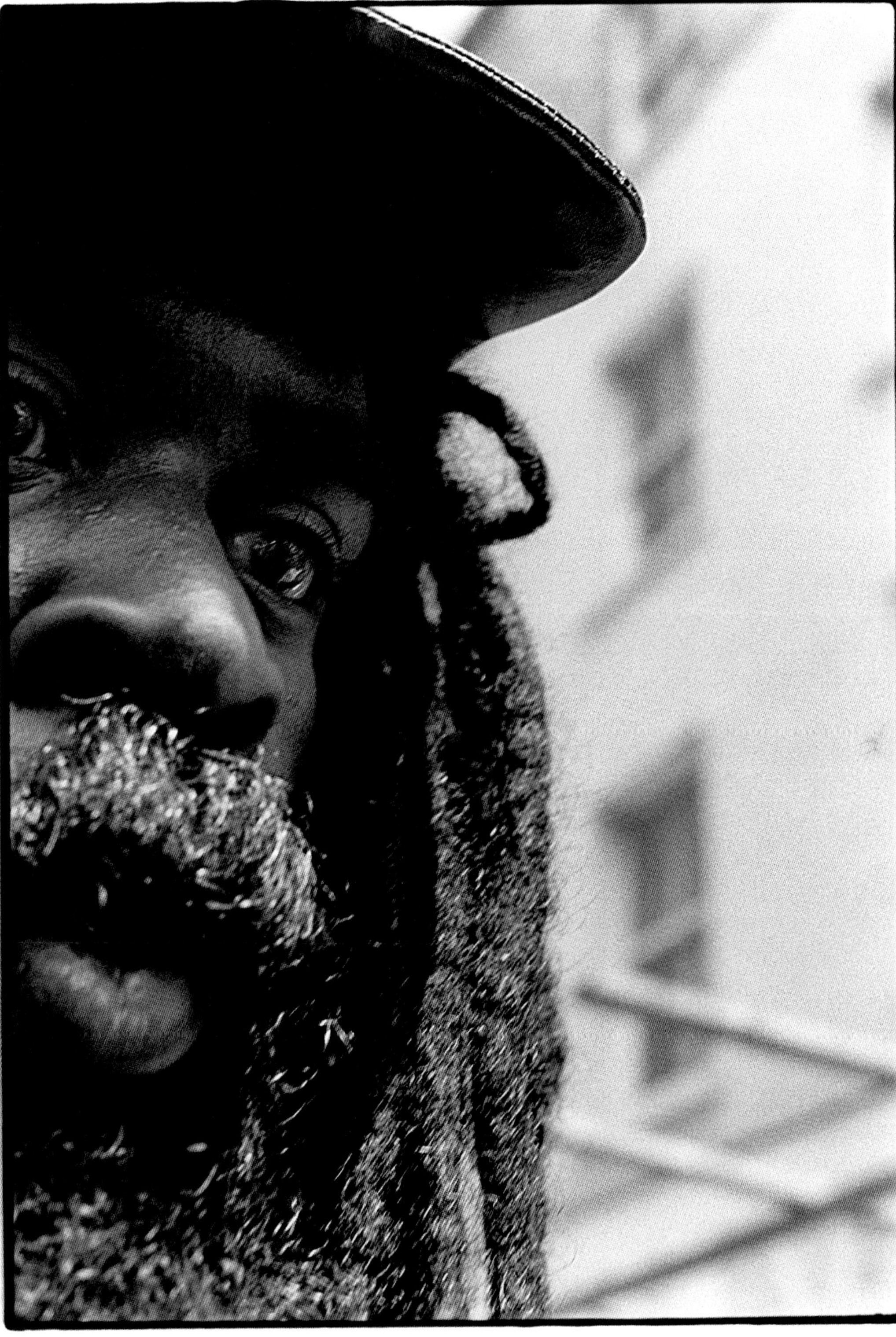

The City, 1989

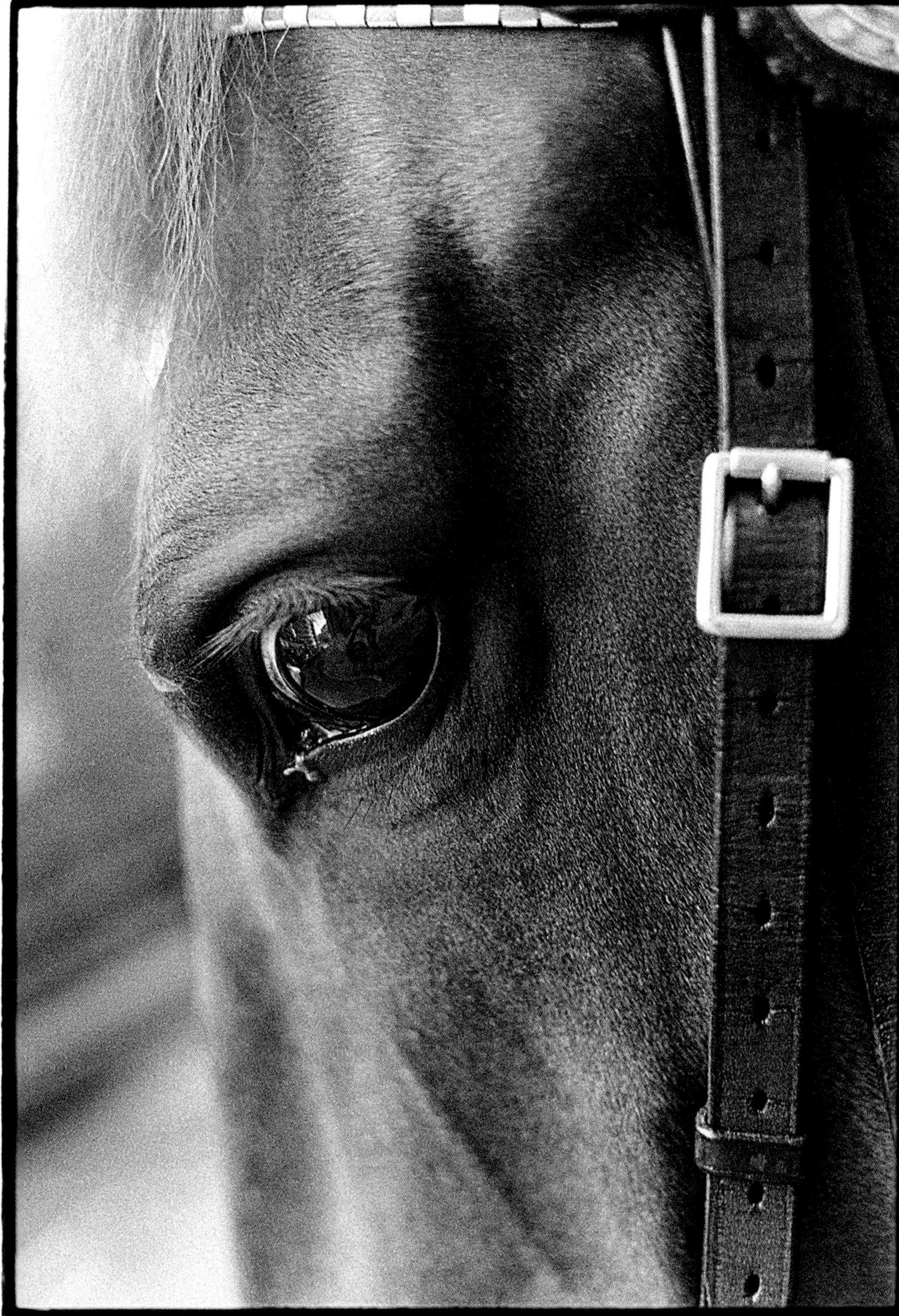

Brick Lane, 1982

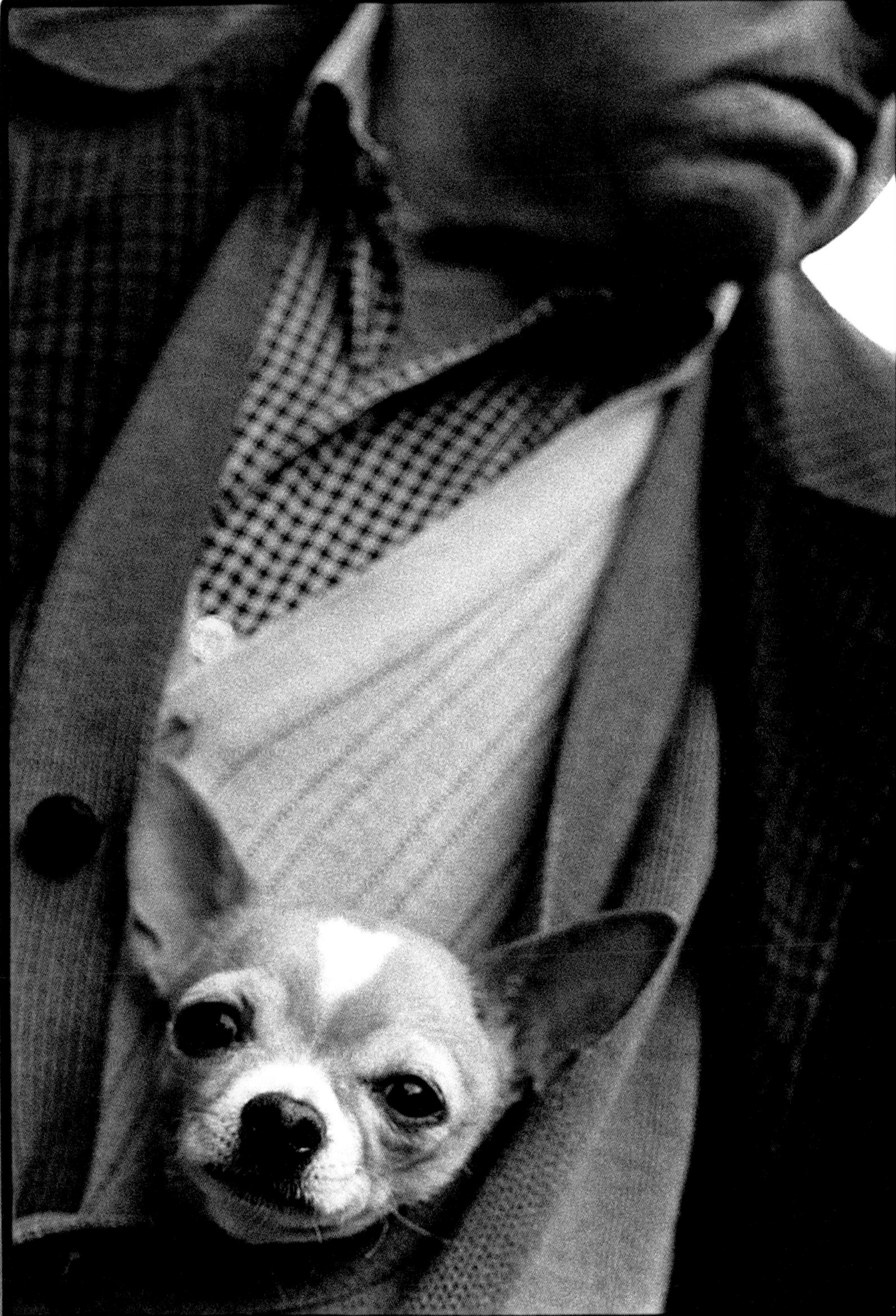

The City, 1989

Overleaf: Brick Lane, 1989 and 1982

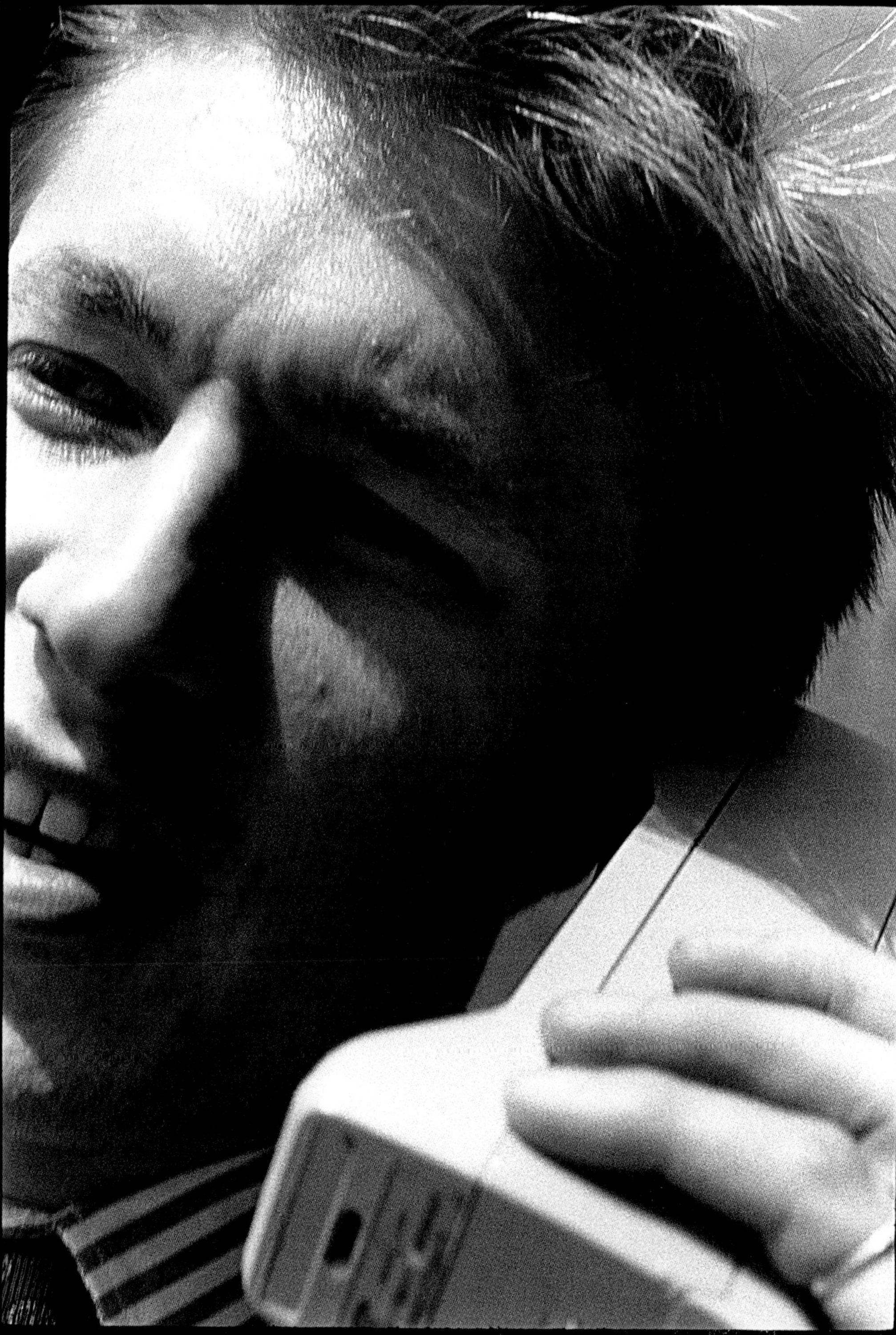

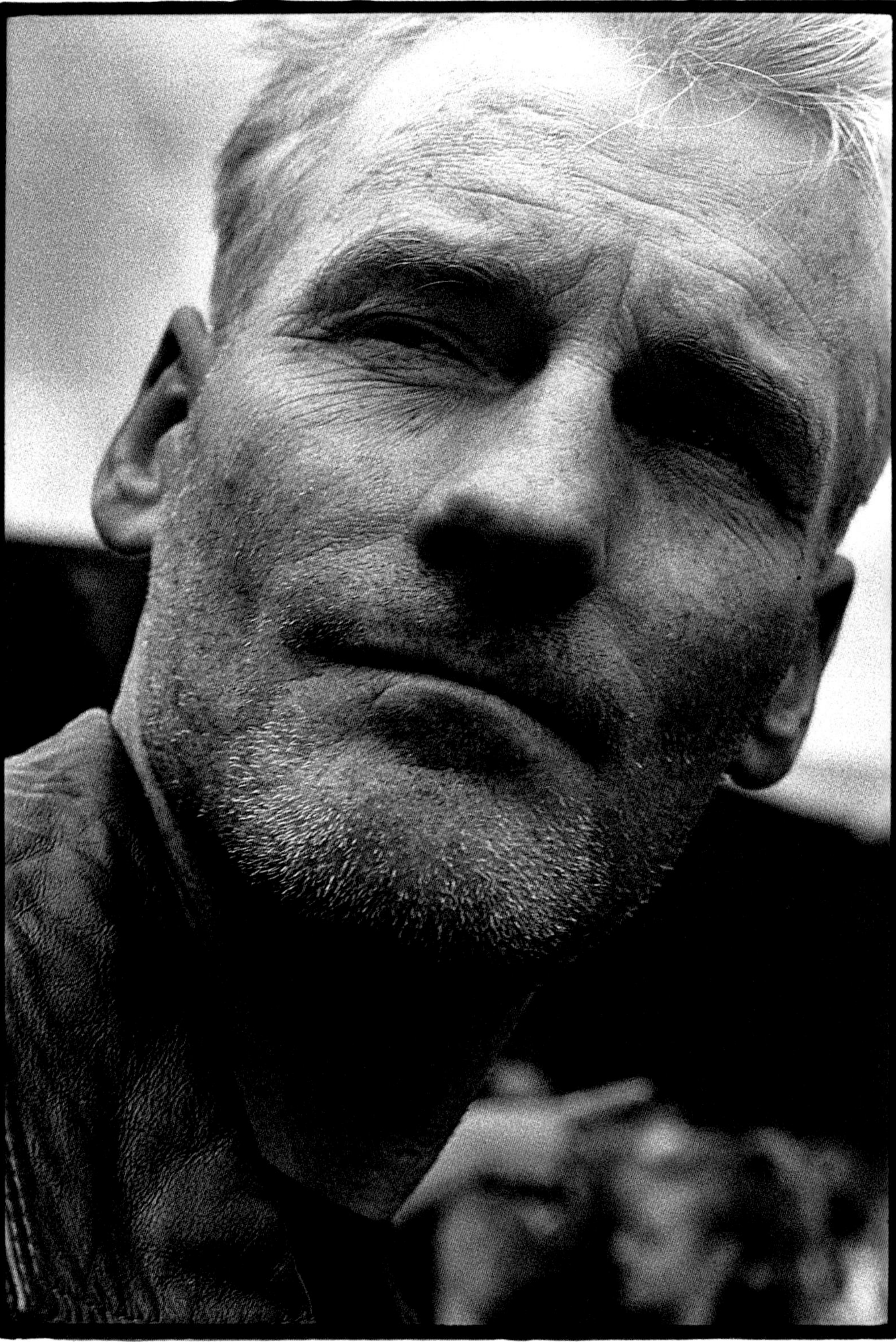

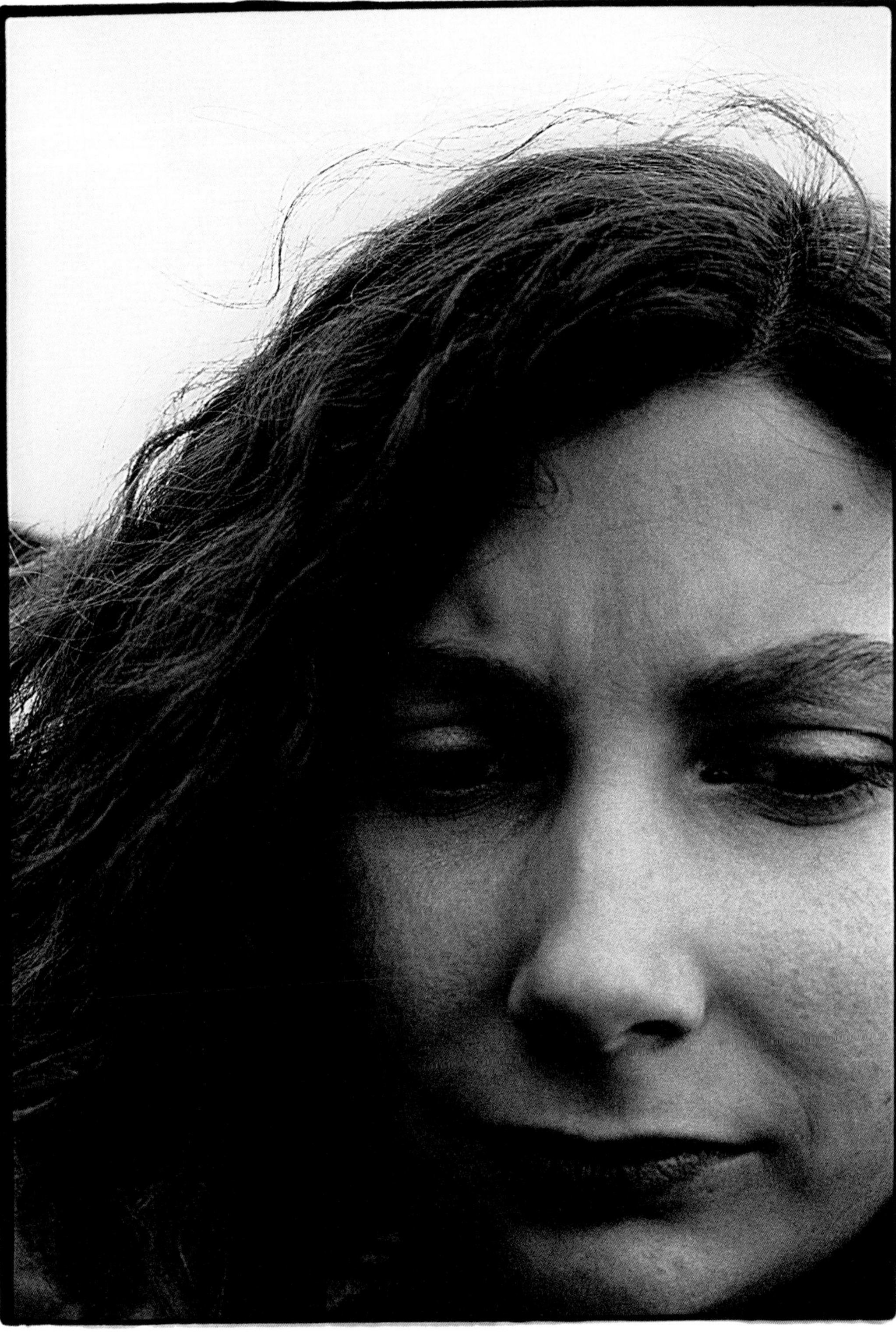

The City, 1992

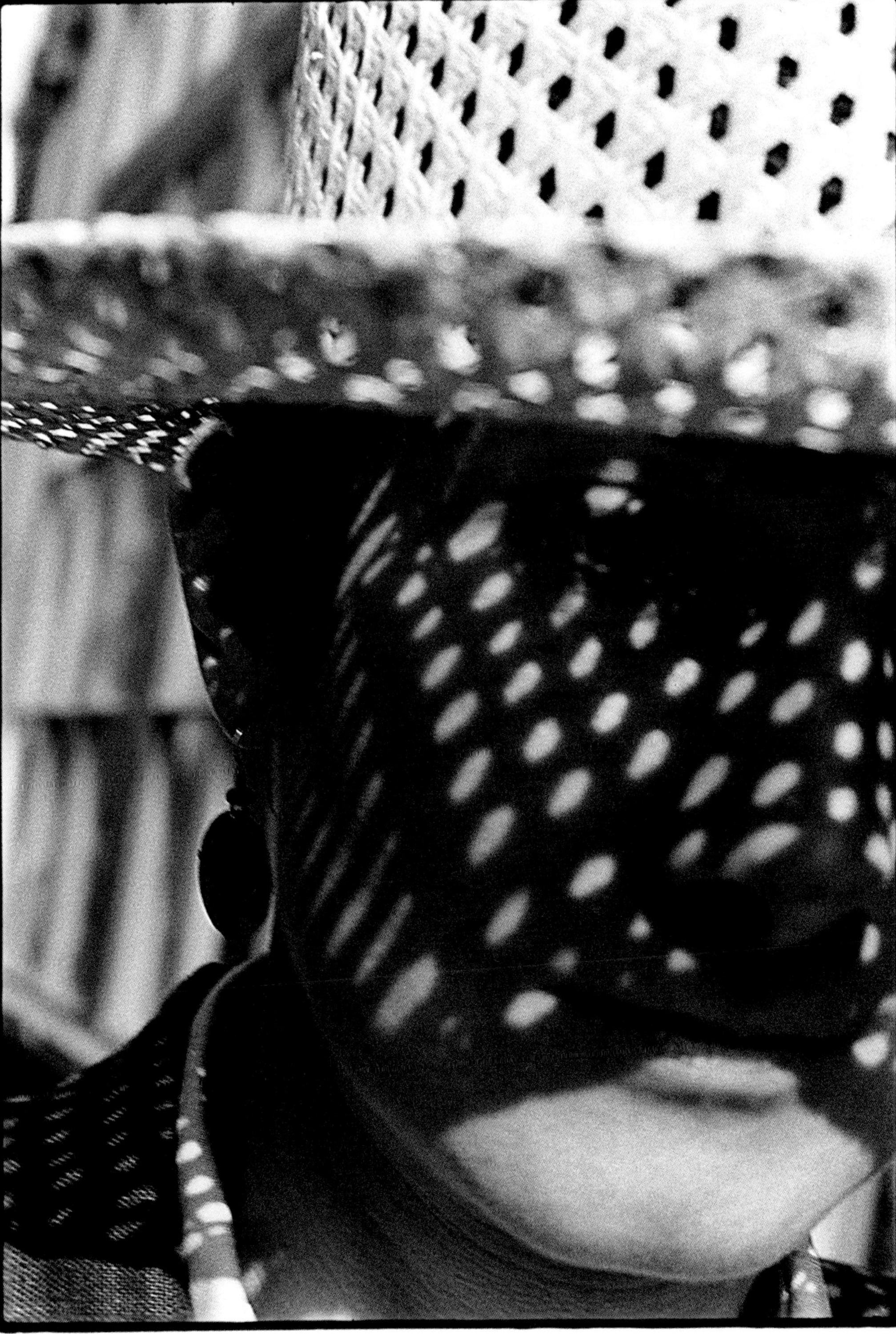

Brick Lane, 1983

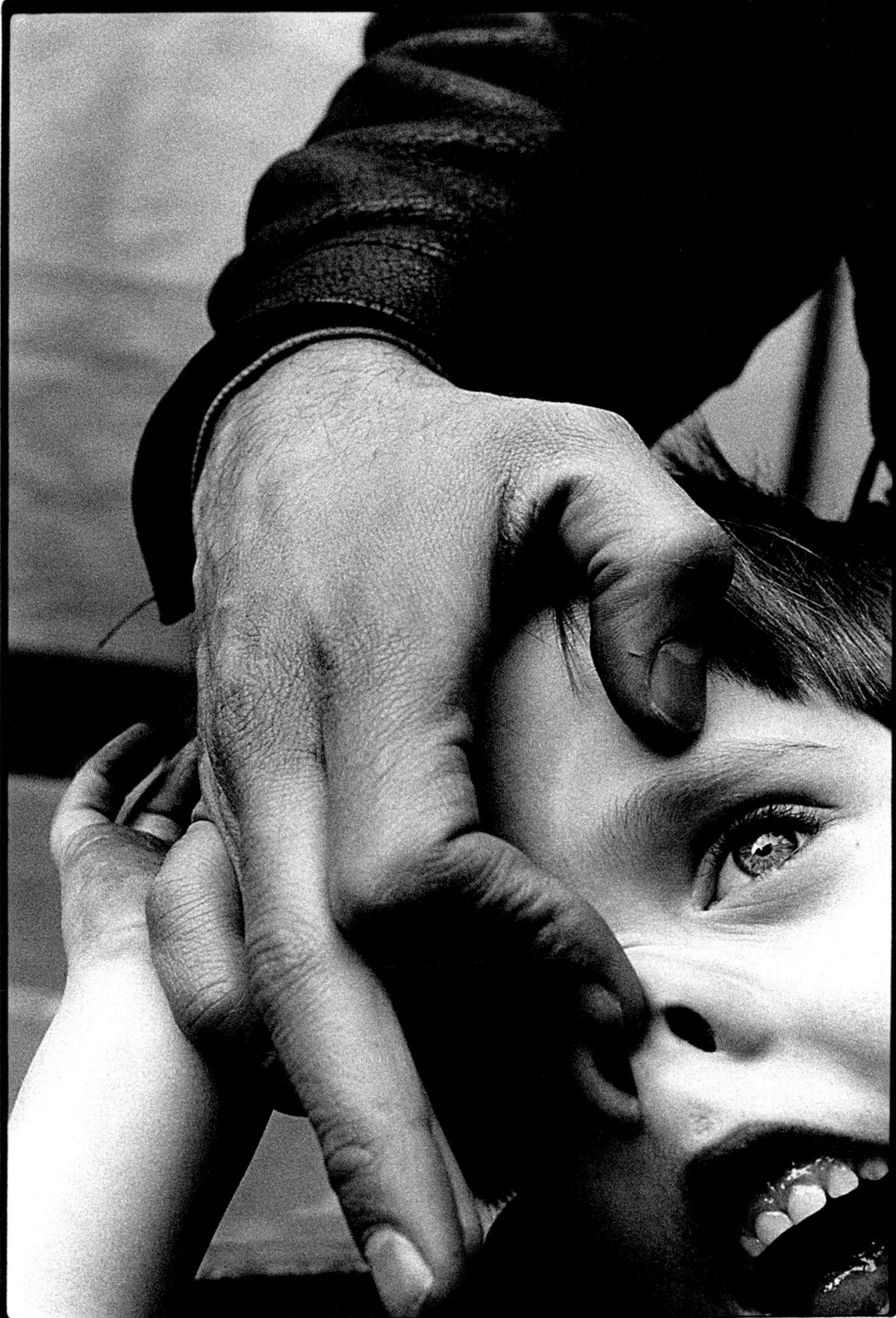

The City, 1989

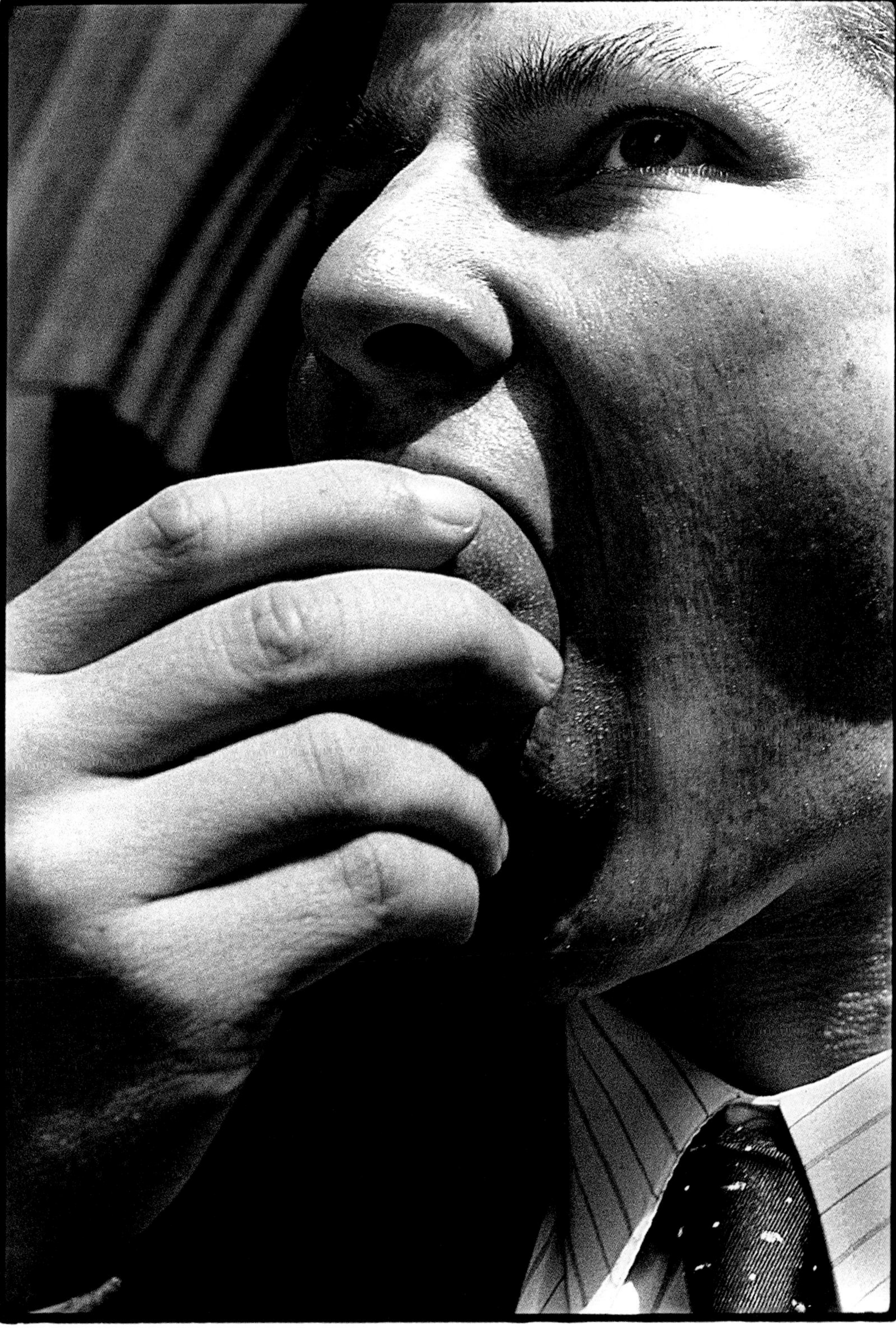

Brick Lane, 1982

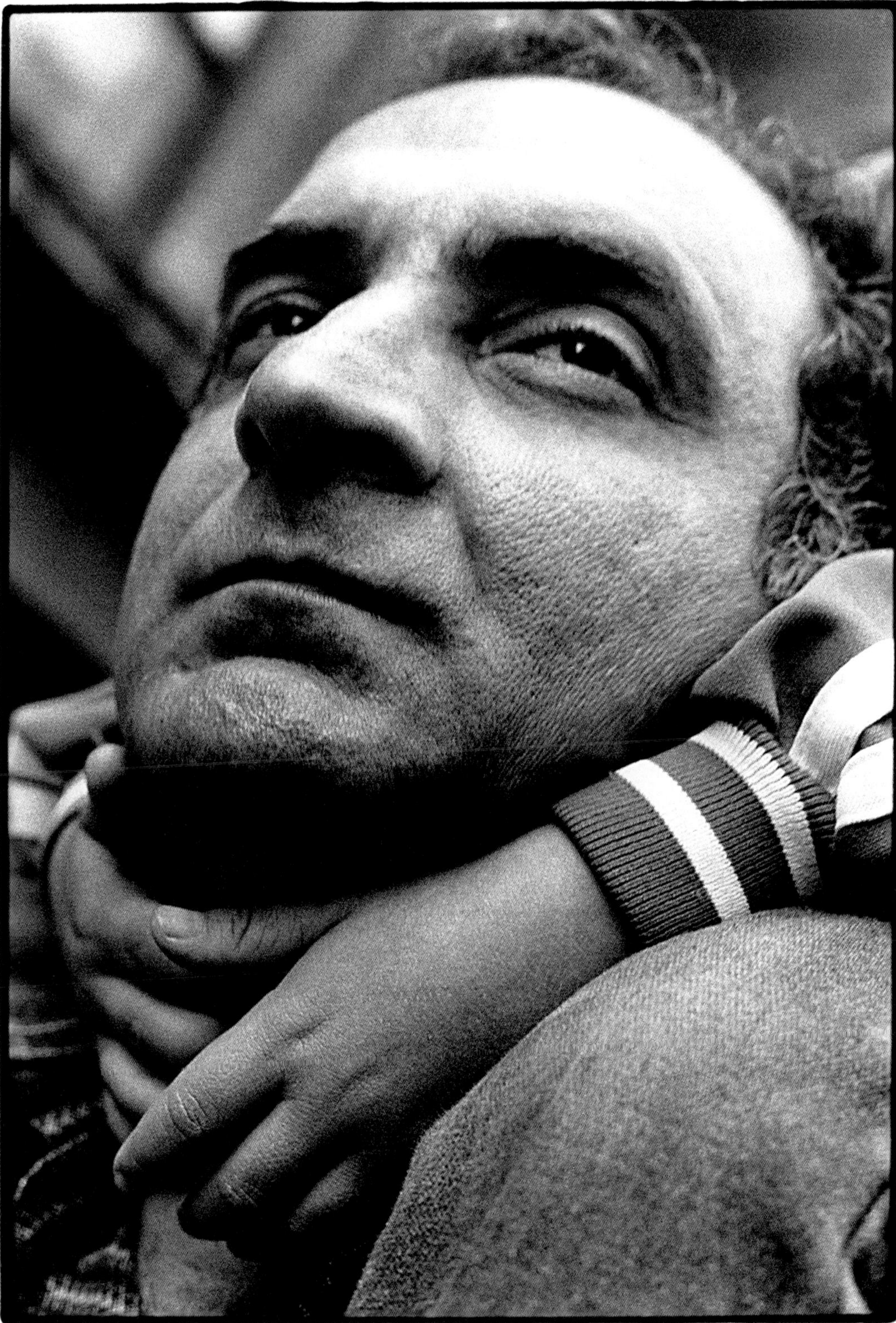

The City, 1991

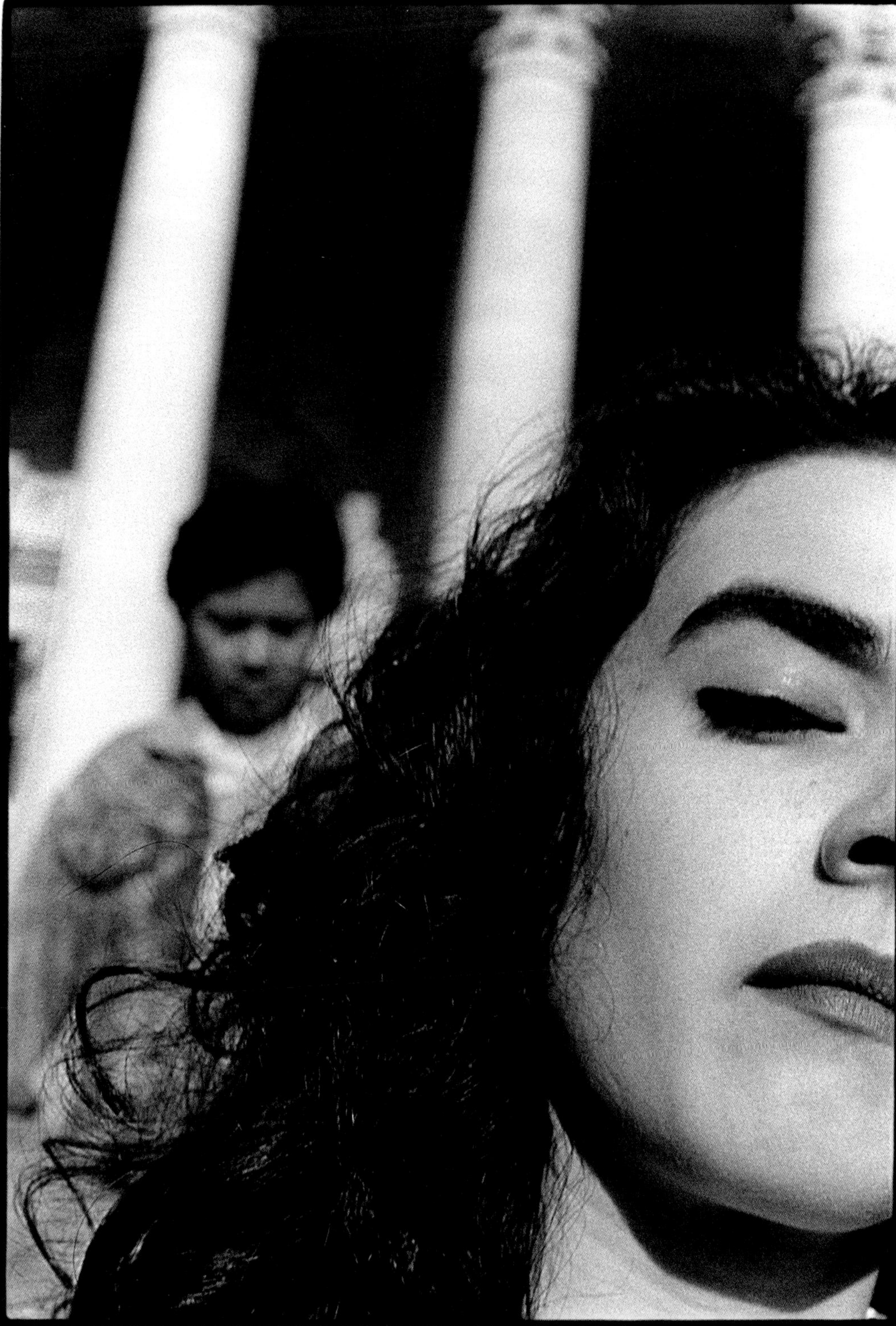

Brick Lane, 1982

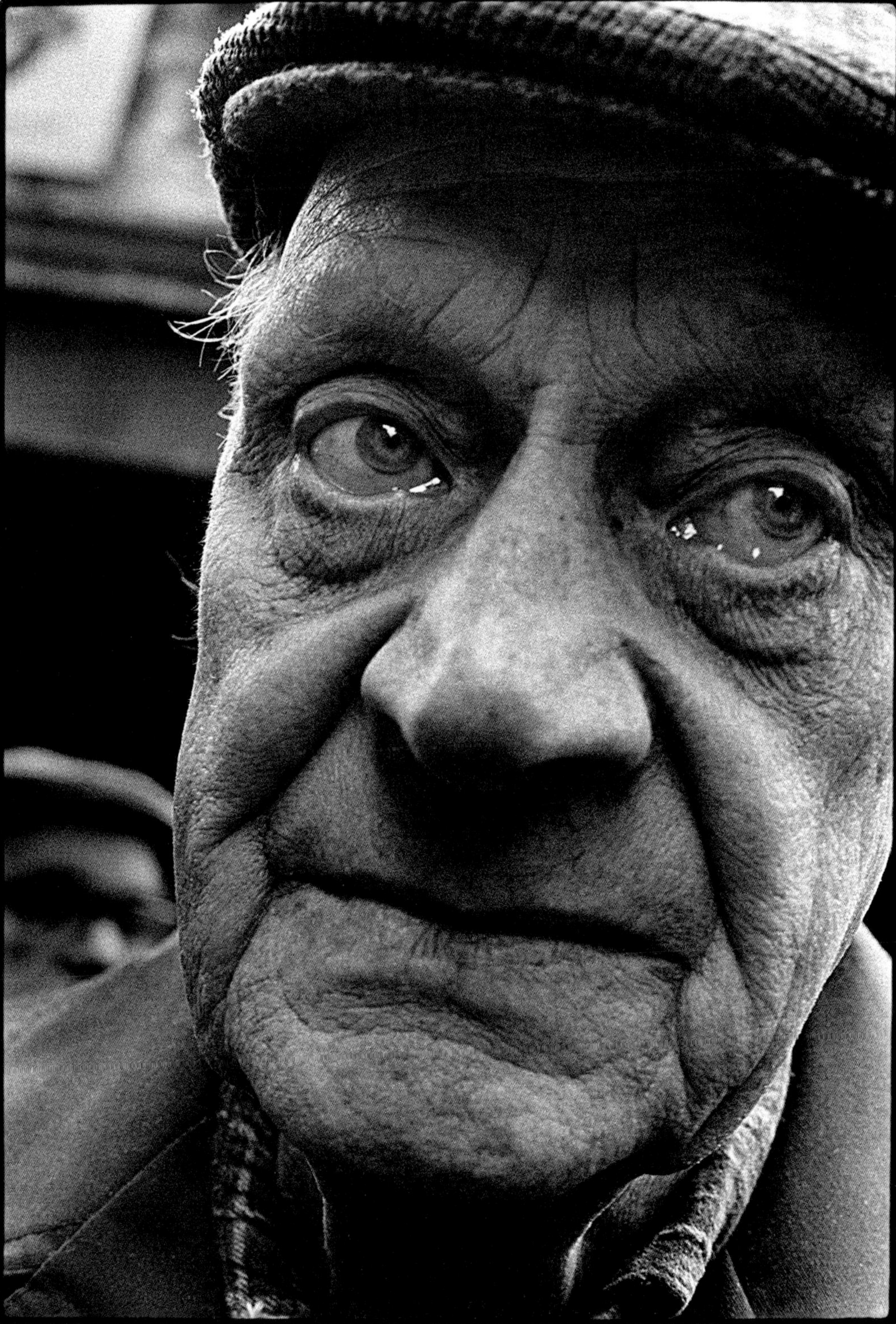

The City, 1989

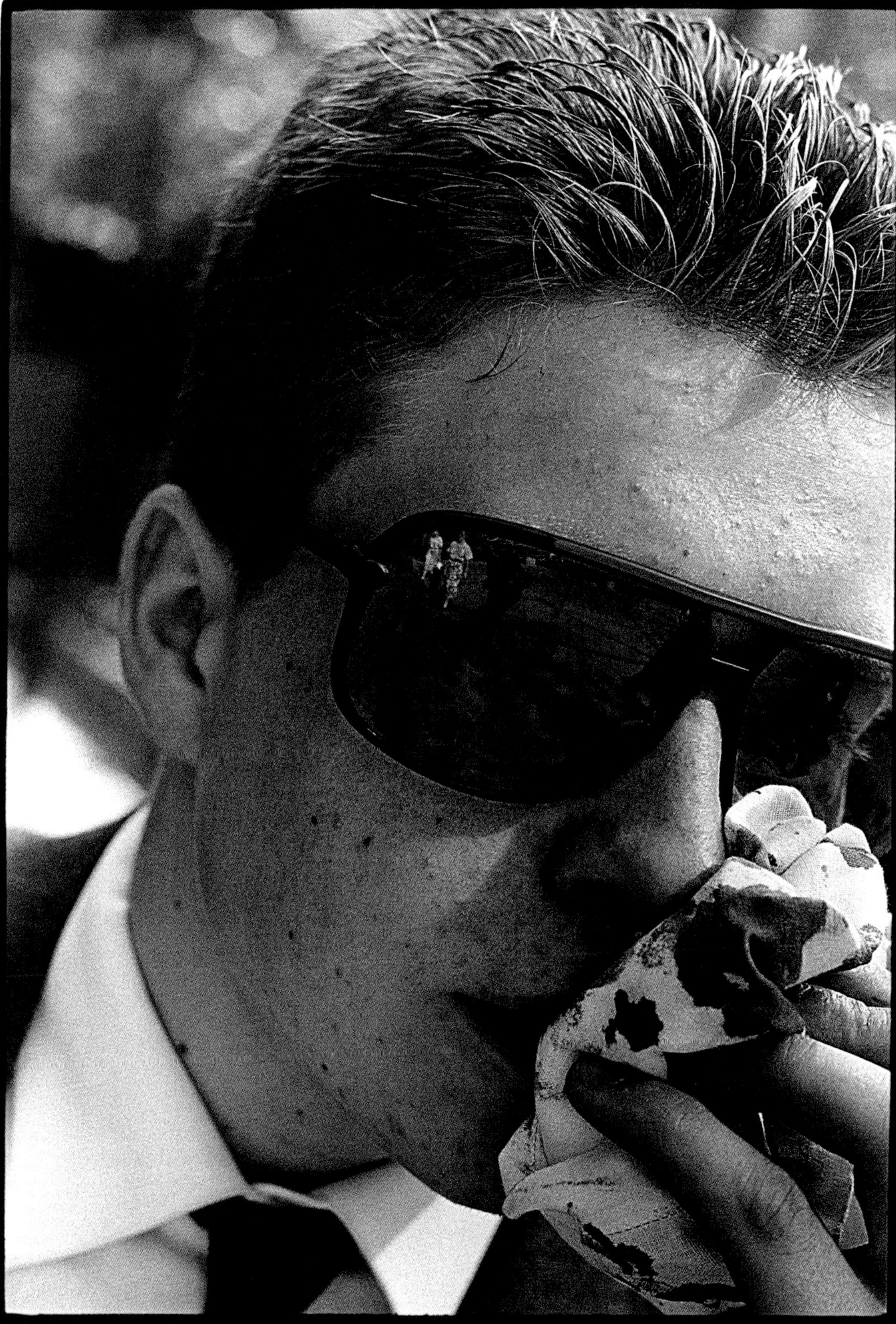

Brick Lane, 1982

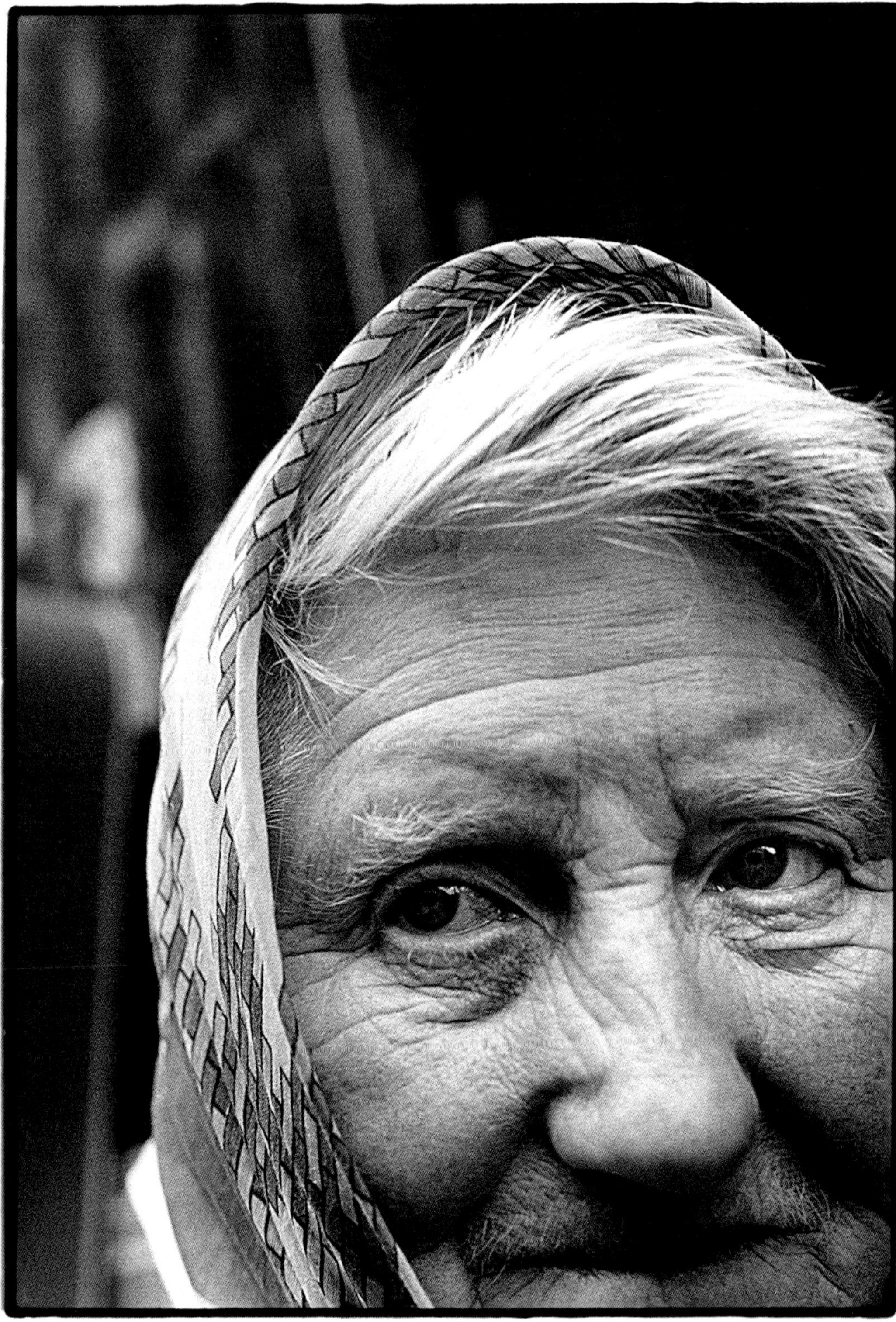

The City, 1989

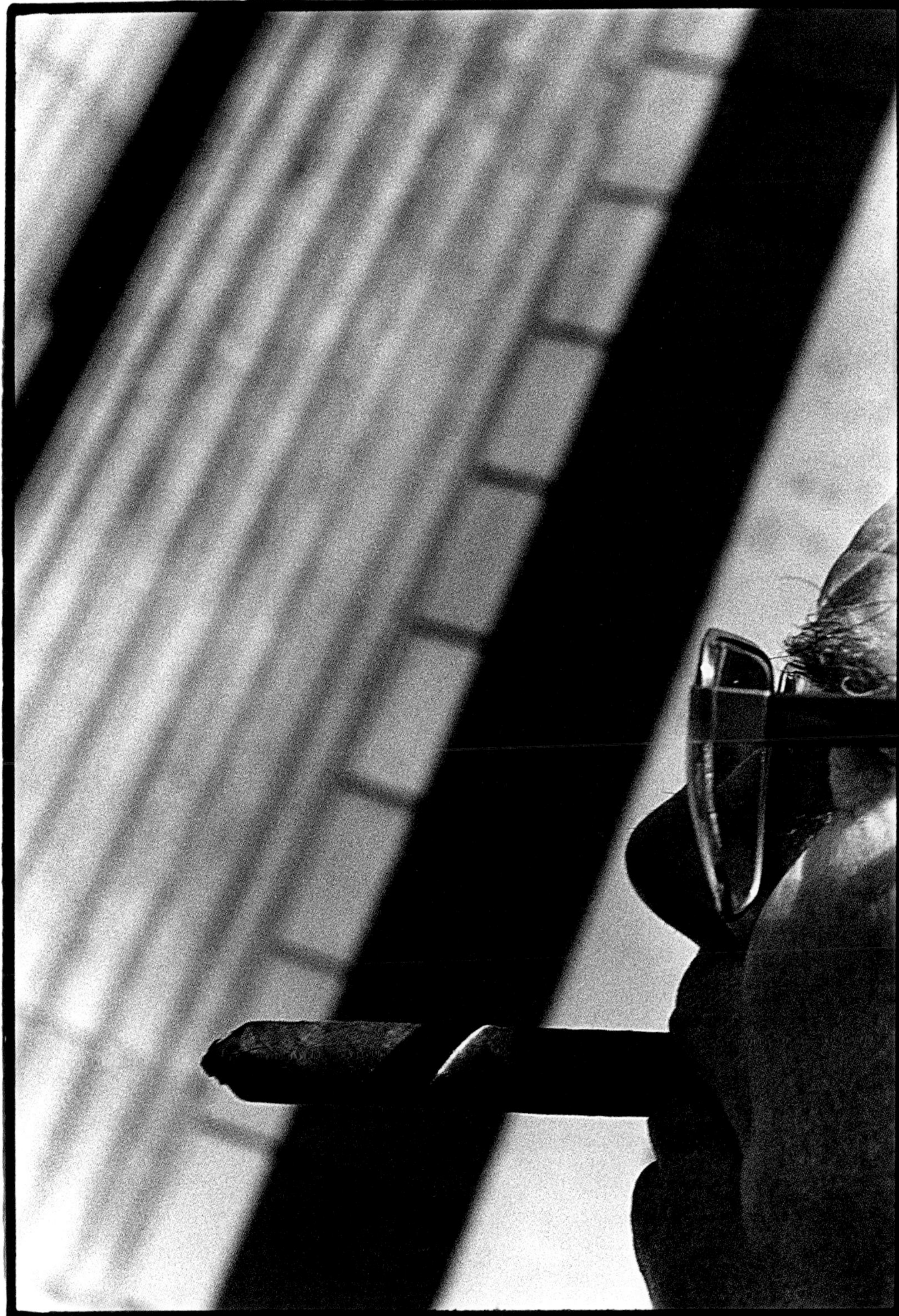

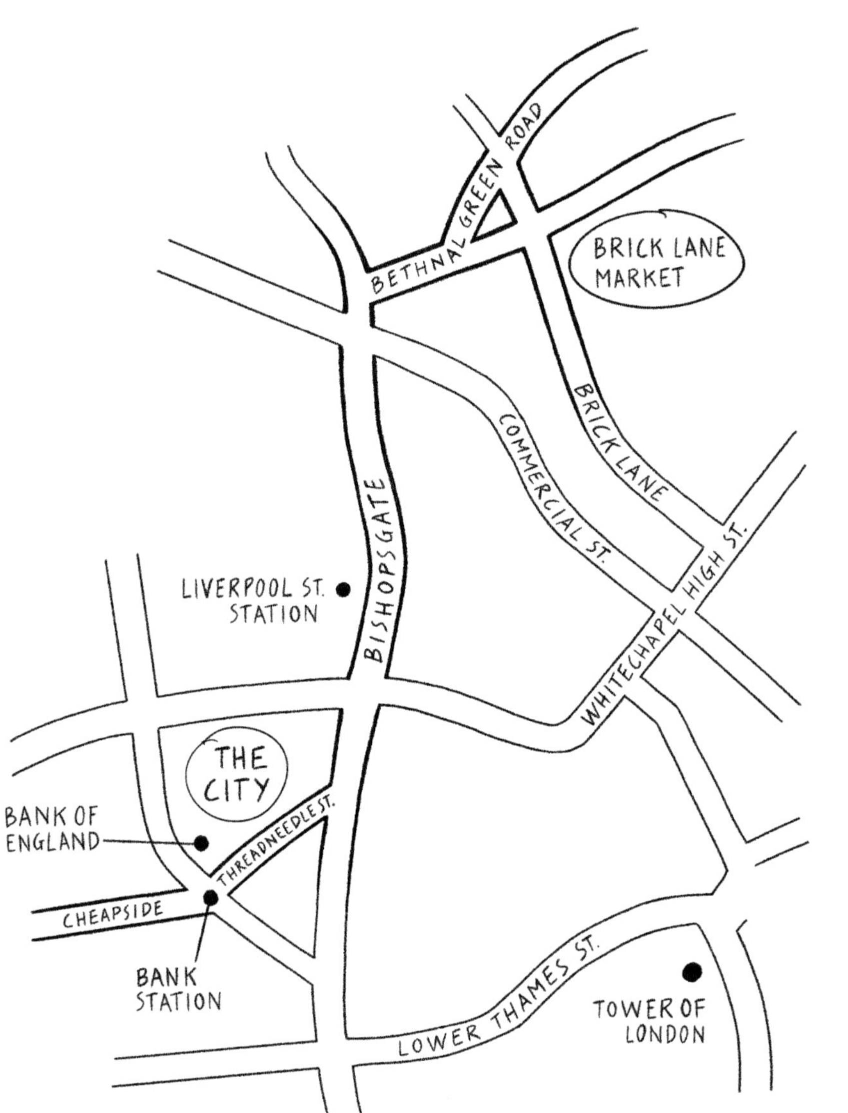

BETHNAL GREEN ROAD
BRICK LANE MARKET
BRICK LANE
COMMERCIAL ST.
BISHOPSGATE
LIVERPOOL ST. STATION
WHITECHAPEL HIGH ST.
THE CITY
THREADNEEDLE ST.
BANK OF ENGLAND
CHEAPSIDE
BANK STATION
LOWER THAMES ST.
TOWER OF LONDON

PROJECT BACKGROUND

In Your Face is reproduced from prints made in Paul Trevor's darkroom 30 years ago. He had modified the enlarger's negative holder to make it bigger than the negatives, hence the photographs' black borders.

The project was shot largely in the 1980s, provoked by Thatcherism and a polarised debate on market forces versus community values. But it was in 1977 that Paul Trevor first tested his new close-up approach. Intrigued by the results, but lacking time to continue, a handful of prints were pinned to the wall so they would not be forgotten. They stayed there for five years! In 1982 he resumed shooting in the Brick Lane market. A commission from Channel 4 in 1989 enabled him to extend the project to The City, and funding from the Cross Channel Photographic Mission in 1991 helped him to complete the series.

After exhibitions at the Blue Sky Gallery, Portland, Oregon in 1991, Hove Museum & Art Gallery, 1993, and the Royal Festival Hall, London, 1994, a book was planned. But back then publication of books by little-known photographers depended on Arts Council support, which the Photography Panel declined to give in 1994, '95 and '96. Despite these setbacks, photographer and friend Josef Koudelka persuaded Paul Trevor to continue editing the photographs.

In 1998 a triptych-style book dummy was made, accompanied by an online app inviting people to offer editing suggestions. (*In Your Face: A Book in the Making* at http://www.ellipsis.net/face/info.html). Thereafter the project stalled until it was introduced to new audiences by Stephen McLaren in 2016 and Martin Parr in 2018.

ACKNOWLEDGEMENTS

This book has been a long time coming. My appreciation is in two parts.

First, I'm pleased to finally be able to record my thanks to those who supported the project in the 1980s and '90s, when no publisher could be found for it: Anna Arnone, who printed many of the project photographs as my darkroom assistant in the 1980s. Edward Barber, Chris Killip and Josef Koudelka, who offered generous feedback and encouragement. Peter Brawne, who supported efforts to get the work published. Chris Rauschenberg, who organised an exhibition of the work in the USA in 1991. Leo Stable, who organised exhibitions of the work in the UK in 1993 and 1994. Jonathan Moberly, for his collaboration in producing the interactive app *In Your Face: A Book in the Making* in 1998, and for continuing to host it.

Second, for the re-emergence of the work in recent years, my grateful thanks to: Stephen McLaren, for his encouragement to re-engage with the project in 2016, and for his Introduction. Martin Parr, for his enthusiastic support and exhibiting the work at his Foundation in 2018, and Louis Little, for his cheerful collaboration in printing the show. Mike Goldwater, for his perceptive feedback on the editing of the book. Martin, Ann, Anna, Faith and Daniele at Hoxton Mini Press, for a superb collaboration despite the pandemic and everyone having to work from home.

Paul Trevor
May 2020

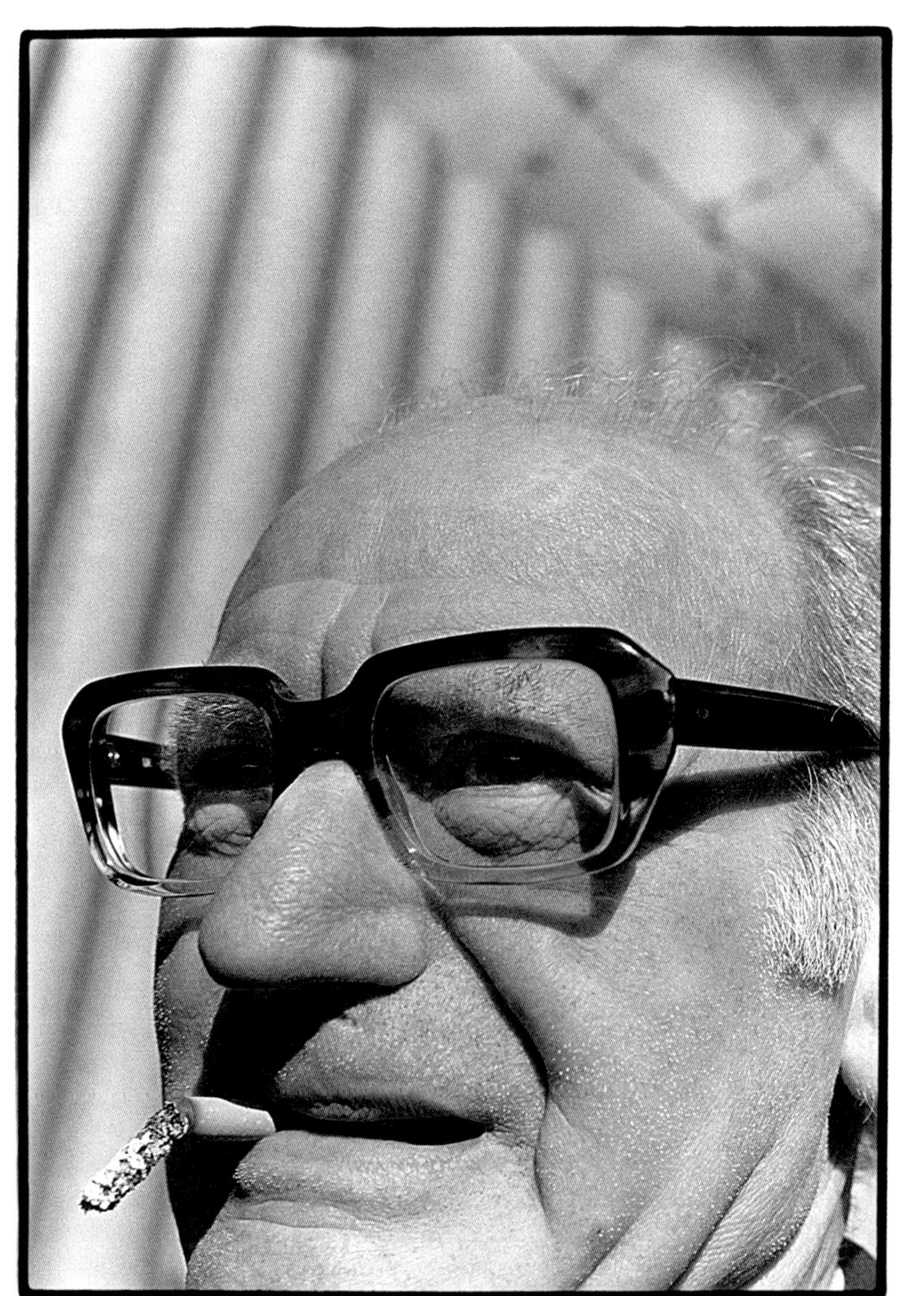

PAUL TREVOR

Paul Trevor is a self-taught photographer who abandoned his job as an
accountant when he was 25. A storyteller at heart, photography offered tools
which he embraced with enthusiasm. Motivated by a keen social impulse,
he applied to picture-making the rapid hand-eye coordination he acquired
as a teenage table tennis ace.

In Your Face is the second book of his projected Eastender series. Each
publication is planned to be distinctively different. The first book,
Once Upon a Time in Brick Lane, was published in 2019 by Hoxton Mini Press.

Paul Trevor's photographs have been exhibited internationally since the
1970s and are in public and private collections worldwide.

www.paultrevor.com

HOXTON MINI PRESS

We are a small, award-winning independent publisher based in east London, not very far from either The City or Brick Lane. We make collectable photography books about local, human stories (many of which are about Hackney). Crucially, our books are accessible: high quality but easy to buy and to enjoy.

As the world goes ever more online we believe that books should be cherished as beautiful, physical objects that earn their place on well-managed shelves and are then passed down through generations.

Hoxton Mini Press was started by Ann and Martin, and their two dogs, Moose and Bug, all of whom live in east London.

www.hoxtonminipress.com

In Your Face

First edition

Copyright © Hoxton Mini Press 2020. All rights reserved.

Photographs © Paul Trevor
Introduction © Stephen McLaren
Photo editing: Paul Trevor
Text editing: Faith McAllister
Design support and map: Daniele Roa
Production: Anna De Pascale

ISBN 978-1-910566-80-0

A CIP catalogue record for this book is available from the British Library

First published in the United Kingdom in 2020 by Hoxton Mini Press.
No part of this publication may be reproduced, stored in a retrieval
system, or transmitted in any form or by any means, electronic,
mechanical, photocopying, recording or otherwise, without
the prior written permission of the copyright owner.

The moral rights of the author have been asserted in accordance with
sections 77 and 78 of the Copyright, Designs and Patents Act 1988

Printed and bound by: Artron, China

To order books, collector's editions and signed prints please go to:
www.hoxtonminipress.com

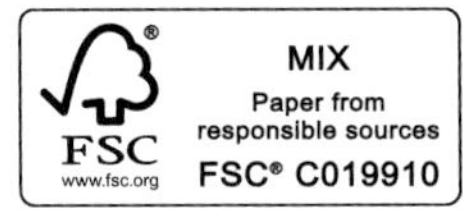